Mermaids

SOPHIA KINGSHILL

A LITTLE TOLLER **MONOGRAPH**

Published by Little Toller Books in 2015

Little Toller Books, Lower Dairy, Toller Fratrum, Dorset

Jacket & frontispiece illustration © Jonny Hannah 2015

CONTENTS

Madrid mermaid, 2013

Introduction

In December 2013, I saw a mermaid in Madrid. She was about four foot long from her waving curls to her tail-fin, scrawled on a wall in red spray paint. Instead of a mirror she had a heart in her hand, next to the feminist symbol of a circle and cross; beneath her was the slogan *Abajo el patriarcado!* – 'Down with patriarchy!' Alongside, another message read: *No dejes a tu vida, sea escenario!* – 'Don't give up on your life, take centre stage!'

To a writer just embarked on a history of mermaids, this was a gift: evidence that my subject was alive and well, and had become an urban warrior. Other recent examples I'd been considering were very different. *Pirates of the Caribbean: On Stranger Tides* (2011) features gorgeous, bloodthirsty beings who drag their prey to the depths to drown and devour them. Then there's the Little Mermaid, who barters her sweet voice in exchange for a fully human form, in order to be with her prince. Whether in Disney's animated adaptation of 1989, as the iconic Copenhagen statue, or in Hans Andersen's 1836 fairytale, she's no man-eater, but all too vulnerable. My Spanish Siren was yet another kettle of fish, neither vamp nor victim, but a self-aware female, angry and confident.

Apart from their tails, these marine sisters are as unalike

as the daughters of King Lear. How are they related? What separates them, and what unites them?

The enduring popularity of mermaids as a cultural phenomenon means that their story spans eras, continents and art forms. The earliest surviving images date from over three thousand years ago; since then, mermaids have been carved in temples and churches, decorated fountains and palaces, and been used as inn signs, figureheads and tattoos. Sightings of fishy humanoids were reported by the first sailors in the Mediterranean and by pioneers to the New World, and are still rumoured around busy modern coasts. Mermaids can be emblems of maritime trade, of the sea's beauty and terror, or of feminine seduction, and legends of water-spirits, both romantic and frightening, are told worldwide.

A mermaid's meaning depends on who's interpreting her. To a mariner, traditionally, she's an omen of storm; poets have employed her as a symbol of fickle womanhood, her sinuous tail meaning she's slippery by nature; a showman might advertise a stuffed specimen as a marvel, to bring in the crowds. Representations change over time, too. Whereas in antiquity, a hybrid woman-fish was an image of a goddess or at least an attendant on the deities of the sea, later iconography made her signify sin and temptation, a metaphor reworked by Pre-Raphaelite artists to whom a Siren was a sexy model.

No possible approach to such richly varied material is straightforward, and my Madrid encounter suggested an angle which, if no simpler than any other, might give a fresh perspective. So direct was that Siren's appeal, her assertion of immediate presence and personality, it seemed to demand that I should take my starting point from

Alan Sorrell, mural painted for the Festival of Britain (1951)

her, the most up-to-date mermaid I'd met, and trace the evolution of the species backwards as you might investigate someone's family tree. Like all families, it's complicated, with great-grandparents on one side turning out to be cousins of a separate branch: the chronology isn't clearcut, and sometimes a thematic explanation is easier to follow than a timeline, but as a rough guide, the opening chapters explore the present and recent past, with several sections focusing on the nineteenth century, the heyday of mermaids in folklore, art and entertainment. From there the story goes back to the Renaissance and Middle Ages, and finally arrives at the ancient world.

Wangechi Mutu, *Beneath Lies the Power* (2014)

One

MODERN MERMAIDS

In 2012, an Internet article identified mermaid novels as the 'hottest new trend' of Young Adult fiction, but concluded that they were unlikely to oust vampires or schoolboy magicians from the bestseller lists 'because they are, to put it bluntly, girls' books'. Of the authors mentioned in the article, one is a man, sixteen are women.

A few of the books cited are actually about sea *boys*, but the article's title refers to mer*maids* alone. This is standard usage, in spite of the fact that mermen have as ancient a presence, in legend and in art, as mermaids. Although witnesses report seeing bearded as well as breasted creatures in the waves, and if merfolk have a gender at all (given their lack of equipment), there's nothing to say that their chromosomes should be more X than Y, the people of the sea are just about unique among creatures real or fabulous, in that the female term covers both sexes: as a collective noun, we're far likelier to talk about 'mermaids' than 'merfolk'. Mermaids, moreover, get more publicity than their he-counterparts. A Google search for 'merman' yields around eight hundred thousand results, 'mermaid' well over twenty million. Males are, for once, the second sex.

That doesn't automatically empower the mermaid: quite the reverse. For most of her history, she's been depicted, described, and voiced by male artists, seafarers, theologians and storytellers, and whether as object of desire or figure of fear, a half-naked woman is, or has been, obviously intended to delight or disquiet a largely male audience.

Now the pendulum's swung the other way, and mermaids are inspiring women not just in Young Adult Fish Lit, but across the media. Artist Wangechi Mutu mounted a London exhibition of paintings, sculpture and video in 2014 under the title *Nguva na Nyoka* (Sirens and Serpents). The *nguva* or dugong is an aquatic mammal that is the equivalent of the Siren in Kenyan coastal legend; Mutu uses images of the *nguva* to explore questions of feminism, ecology and metamorphosis, and contrasts its intense and sometimes savage powers with 'the sanitised mermaid of popular European culture'.

Singer Mariah Carey recorded her 1999 album *Rainbow* in Capri, and in an interview she recalled her pleasure when she saw the Scoglio delle Sirene, 'Sirens' Rock':

The Sirens would sit there and lure in the men. They gave them this rock because women were considered less important than men, and that's their revenge: they sexually entice men with their voices to come to this rock . . . I just fell in love with that.

The idea that the Sirens' magnetism helped them get even with men has obvious relevance to the career of a pop diva like Carey, whose appearance and sexuality are exploited to market her singing.

The mermaid as spokeswoman for equality, typified by the Madrid graffiti I saw in 2013, goes back at least to the

1970s, when the name *Siren* was used for a feminist magazine in Chicago. A pattern has been established of women reclaiming the mermaid, reacting against male-dominated traditions defining her as submissive or seductive.

There are earlier examples of the belligerent mermaid, without any particular sex bias. Warsaw's city crest, which evolved from a bird-legged, scaly monster (a classical Siren, in fact, as described in Chapter 12) to become, by the eighteenth century, a recognisable mermaid with a woman's body and a fish's tail, has remained militant throughout, carrying a shield and brandishing a sword. Between 1811 and 1915, under the Fourth Partition of Poland, the *Syrena*, as she's known, was officially banned, but was displayed in many places as an assertion of the city's identity, and in the Second World War she was adopted as the badge of the Polish II Corps.

Pablo Picasso, visiting a Warsaw apartment block under construction in 1948, drew the *Syrena* on an interior wall, giving her the Communist hammer to hold instead of a sword. This image survives only in photographs, since the mural wasn't universally admired. The first person offered the flat in question refused it, on the grounds that he had small children and the mermaid had bare breasts, while the next (childless) candidates were equally horrified:

It was huge, my God was it huge. Her bosom was like two balloons, the eyes were triangular, at the end of her long, oddly long arm she held a hammer; and she had a short, tapering tail at the back.

After a couple of years, the flat's tenants quietly had their private Picasso whitewashed, but the *Syrena* has continued

Picasso's *Warsaw Syrene* (1948): a worker paints the adjoining wall

to appear as a political symbol, employed by supporters of Solidarity in the 1980s, and more recently by the Warsaw Gay Movement.

The common modern perception of the mermaid, however, is of a whimsical and child-friendly fantasy. This image is based to a great extent on the ubiquitous kitsch spawned by the Disney cartoon: but the Little Mermaid herself is not so wholesome, on closer inspection.

Ariel, as she's christened in the film, is drawn with a girlish figure and a pertly pretty face. Her hair is neither seaweed-green nor princess-golden, but a vibrant red, and she hides her breasts in a bikini top, modest for the family market. Ariel's inquisitive nature leads her to take an interest in the human world, and while people-watching, she falls in love with the young prince Eric. When his ship sinks in a storm she saves his life, but swims away before he can see her. She bargains with the sea-witch Ursula for a spell allowing her to exchange her tail temporarily for a pair of legs, in return giving up her voice, which Ursula magically traps in a shell.

Unless she receives a kiss of true love, the mermaid is told, she must remain in the witch's power forever. The wicked Ursula then transforms herself into an attractive woman, and sings in Ariel's voice to bewitch Eric. True identities are eventually discovered, the witch is killed, and Ariel, having regained her voice and become fully human with the help of her father the sea-king, marries her prince.

The Danish original is an altogether darker affair, with a stern message about redemption through suffering. Early in Andersen's 'Little Mermaid', as in the film, its teenage heroine (here nameless) rescues the prince from a shipwreck.

Then, however, it is not love alone that impels her to beg for a human shape, but the desire for an immortal afterlife. Her grandmother tells her that this can be achieved if a man marries her: at the moment the priest joins their hands, she will be granted a share of her husband's soul.

In order to win her prince and thus her chance of eternal life, the mermaid visits a witch. She is warned that having her tail split into two legs will mean continuous agony – every step she takes will feel as if she is treading on a blade sharp enough to make her bleed – and, moreover, that becoming human is a one-way journey. She will never be a mermaid again.

In payment for her spell, the witch demands the mermaid's voice, which she takes not with a reversible charm, but by cutting out her tongue. Dumb, and in terrible pain, the mermaid reaches the palace, where she is kept as a kind of pet, allowed to sleep on a cushion outside her prince's door. The prince is fond of her, but his love is bestowed on a princess he believes to be the girl who saved him from drowning. He marries the princess, and the mermaid acts as bridesmaid at the wedding.

Her sisters, meanwhile, longing to bring her back to them, have acquired a magic knife from the witch. This, they tell the mermaid, must be plunged into the prince's heart, and his blood will turn her feet back into a fish-tail. She can't bring herself to kill him. Instead she throws the knife into the sea, then dives in herself, and feels her body melt into foam, a mermaid's death.

Nevertheless she does not die, but is transformed into a spirit of the air, who can gain a soul by three centuries of good deeds. One of her ethereal companions tells her that for every good child she visits, the three hundred years will be

Edmund Dulac, *The Little Mermaid Saved the Prince* (1911)

shortened by one year, but at the sight of a naughty child she will cry, and every tear shed will add a day to her probation.

The religious trappings do have a certain authority behind them. Medieval theologians had speculated as to whether mermaids and other 'monsters' possessed souls, and some concluded that a mermaid did not, but wished she did. The idea that she could gain one by marrying a human being was proposed by earlier authors than Andersen, and the Little Mermaid's metamorphosis into an airy form is based on philosophical concepts of the four elements, earth, fire, water, and air.

The physical and emotional torments that the mermaid undergoes are Andersen's own invention, and however unpleasant to read, they are what gives the story its power both as tragic romance and as parable of a female rite of passage. Writing for children in the early nineteenth century, Andersen could not say straight out that in order to be a man's wife, the mermaid would have to be able to have sex, and therefore must have sex organs. Instead, he has the wise grandmother point out that humans consider tails ugly, hence the need for legs. Then, whether intentionally or not, he invests the splitting of the mermaid's tail with all the pain and secret mess of puberty and loss of virginity, her feet standing in for what in a woman is hidden and below. Wordless, in pain though no one sees you bleeding, unrequitedly in love, longing for a better world than this one: what adolescent can't identify?

Sadistic and didactic, the tale makes uneasy reading, and one can readily understand Disney's changes to make the plot palatable, but it was widely loved long before his studios got their hands on it. Operas and ballets have been based on it, Shirley Temple starred in it on television, and comic-book, manga and anime versions have been produced. Illustrations have tended to emphasise the Mermaid's virginal purity and wistful charm, although one sketch by Lorenz Frølich hides her breasts but gives her a suggestively cleft bum above her fishtail.

Lorenz Frølich's sketch of 'The Little Mermaid' (1837)

Most famous of all visual interpretations must be the statue which has become a national symbol of Copenhagen. After seeing a ballet based on Andersen's tale, Carl Jacobsen, head of Carlsberg Breweries and a great patron of the arts, commissioned Edvard Eriksen's sculpture, which was unveiled in 1913. Eriksen wanted to give his Little Mermaid legs, but Jacobsen held out for a tail, and a compromise was reached: the Copenhagen mermaid has clearly defined thighs, knees and calves, terminating in two large graceful fins. The sculptor may have realised how vital it was for Andersen's heroine to be a forked animal – although locals have explained the legs as allowing their Mermaid to ride a bicycle, like the rest of the Danes. In fact the double-tailed mermaid is not a novelty, but a very old motif, as we'll see.

Despite being visited and admired by countless tourists,

Edvard Eriksen, *The Little Mermaid* (1913)

the Copenhagen Little Mermaid, like her fairytale original, has suffered. In 1964, her head was sawn off, although it was quickly replaced using a cast from the original model. An arm was removed in 1984, she was decapitated again in 1998, and in 2003 she was blown right off her base by an explosive charge, while more superficial damage has been achieved with paint.

At least some of this vandalism has been motivated by

protest. In one of the latest episodes, *March* 8 – the date of International Women's Day – was painted on the Mermaid, and she was given a dildo to hold. You could say she's an obvious target for feminist re-interpretation. Andersen's Little Mermaid is a willing sacrifice, both to the insensitive prince, and more importantly to the Church, which denies her a soul except at the cost of anguish.

Older than either the radical or the meek mermaid is the rapacious variety, of which the fearsome creatures who appear in *Pirates of the Caribbean* are recent avatars. The film does feature one 'good' mermaid who falls in love with a human being, but the rest of the breed are carnivorous and merciless. At their first appearance, a couple of nymphs raise heads and arms from the sea to beguile a boatful of sailors with their sweet voices and youthful faces; then the picture pulls back, to reveal more and more converging on the boat like minnows to bait, and finally we see shoals of them leaping around their terrified prey.

On dry land they appear as luscious women, legs and all (what's between is never on display, and their breasts are obscured by long hair), but underwater they are seen to have tails, and fanged mouths like vampires. Although they use their sex to entice, they only want men as food.

Much of this, including their appetite to consume men in the literal sense, is long-standing legend. Homer's Sirens – who are not mermaids at all, as explained later, but who significantly inform the tradition – strew their surroundings with human bones. Themes of homicide and lust intertwine from an early date: a work of the third or second century BC, purporting to record the adventures of Alexander the

Glynis Johns in *Miranda* (1948)

Great in India, mentions women living immersed in a river, who were beautiful – 'Their complexion was snow-white, like nymphs their hair spread over their backs' – but who suffocated Alexander's soldiers during or after the act of love.

A thirteenth-century encyclopedia (in sixteenth-century translation from Latin) describes the Siren as temptress and cannibal:

a beast of the sea wonderfully shapen as a maid from the navell upward, and a fish from the navell downeward, and this wonderfull beast is gladde and merrie in tempest, and sadde and heavie in fayre weather. With sweetnesse of song this beast maketh shipmen to sleepe, and when shee seeth that they be a

Frederick Leighton, *The Fisherman and the Syren* (*c.*1856–58): the young man is helpless, as the mermaid wraps her tail round his legs and her arms round his neck

sleepe, she goeth into the ship, and ravisheth which she may take with her, and bringeth him into a drye place, and maketh him first lye by her, and doe the deede of lechery, and if he will not or may not, then she slaieth him and eateth his flesh.

Pirates of the Caribbean presents an authentic characterisation, and an unusually forthright one for the cinema. More commonly, films have expressed a mermaid's predatory nature in terms of seduction: in *Miranda* (1948), Glynis Johns's character creates emotional havoc among her string of suitors before returning to the sea, and in *Splash!* (1984), Madison (Daryl Hannah) ultimately takes her lover (Tom Hanks) under the waves with her. Although this is presented as a happy ending, it's made clear that he can never come back to the world of humans.

It's always a risk to meet a mermaid.

Two
A PIECE OF TAIL

In the erotically charged context of Victorian and Edwardian art, mermaids appear over and over again, both the dangerous variety and the guileless Hans Andersen model. Representative of the former, Edward Burne-Jones's *The Depths of. the Sea* shows a muscular Siren dragging a naked man to the seabed. She stares out at us, with an enigmatic smile. The strong vertical lines of the picture – even her tail is extended straight down, the fin just curving away as it hits bottom – suggest how far she's pulled him under, and how fast. His beautiful body reclines against and over her, limp, although the upward thrust of her arm round his loins hints that he may still have uses as a sex toy: unless, that is, she's simply going to eat him. Whatever the plans for her prey, this Siren's in control.

William Waterhouse's much-reproduced *Mermaid* is alone, except for us, and seems unaware of the gaze she invites, except that her pose – so perfectly presented for delectation, her tail wrapped shyly around herself, one nipple just visible as she displays her hair – tells us she's complicit in the voyeur's fantasy. This, at all events, is how the (male) artist portrays her to the (male) viewer.

There's another possible reading, though. A turn-of-the-century art-gallery audience would have been familiar with stories of sea-nymphs tempting men only to destroy them, through contemporary prose and poetry where the irresistible, cold-hearted Siren was an immediately recognisable figure. In *Vanity Fair* (1848), Thackeray likens his anti-heroine Becky Sharp to one of the breed:

> They look pretty enough when they sit upon a rock, twangling their harps and combing their hair, and sing, and beckon to you to come and hold the looking-glass; but when they sink into their native element, depend on it, those mermaids are about no good, and we had best not examine the fiendish marine cannibals, revelling and feasting on their wretched pickled victims.

By giving his pretty wench a tail and calling her a mermaid, Waterhouse may imply that she's less innocent than she looks. The watcher is her potential ravisher, but could just be her next victim.

The essence of these nymphs, whether lively or languorous, is their sexuality. At a time when it was taboo to display genitalia in art, a mermaid could be shown 'entirely naked' yet 'decent'. She is the nineteenth-century equivalent of a Page 3 girl, exposed above but unavailable below.

Much of the mermaid's legend centres on her ambivalence. She's presented as a seducer, yet obviously, given that she is woman only down to her waist and fish below, she cannot achieve intercourse. Arousing but never satisfying desire, she is a tease, an unobtainable flirt. Is she herself frustrated? Perhaps her fish-tail, which can appear phallic, means that in some hermaphrodite way she is able to gain pleasure from her own body. In that case, she and the man she ensnares would be mutually masturbatory figures in each other's amorous dreams.

Left: Edward Burne-Jones, *The Depths of the Sea* (1886)
Right: William Waterhouse, *The Mermaid* (1900)

As well as the paradoxical tail, certain other attributes are shared by many pictorial mermaids. Just about all of them have long hair, which fulfils a double or even triple function. Representationally, it is beauty's crowning glory, and since in the nineteenth century a man would generally see a woman with her hair down only in the most intimate setting, its streaming length implies again, however falsely, her availability. Symbolically, it represents the sea's waves,

Evelyn de Morgan, *Sea Maidens* (1886): unlike her male
contemporaries, de Morgan shows the marine sisterhood
as mutually supportive, neither coy nor menacing

emphasising the kinship between the nymph and her
element. Practically, moreover, it hides whatever the artist
would rather not show, a convention still employed today, as
in *The Pirates of the Caribbean*.

If you have long hair, you need to groom it, but the
mermaid's traditional comb and looking glass might not
just be fashion aids. It has been proposed that her mirror
represents the moon, always associated with the sea as well
as with women and their cycles, and that the comb was
originally the plectrum with which the musical Siren once
plucked her lyre.

Alternatively, or additionally, it may be relevant that both
the Greek for comb, *kteis*, and the Latin, *pecten*, can also refer

to the pudenda. In art, a comb traditionally appeared as a symbol of woman's sexuality; on early Christian monuments, the double motif of comb-and-mirror signifies the female gender, and it seems intuitively reasonable that it performs the same function for the mermaid, reinforcing her status as archetypally self-titivating woman.

Before the nineteenth century, the fishtailed mermaid was not much painted, appearing mostly in sculpture, carving and book illustration. Nereids – nymphs aquatic by nature but fully human in shape – were more common in both classical and Renaissance art, although tritons, sea-males with tails, were often shown. Victorian and later painters drew on all these traditions for their sea-women, showing both the tailed and tailless species. A fairly spurious distinction was drawn by some art critics of the time between the fatal mermaid-Siren, who lured men to their doom with her song and her beauty, and the innocent 'ondine', who merely adorned the sea. Ondines generally had legs, could therefore presumably enter into a full sexual relationship, and thus posed less of an emasculatory threat. The categories were by no means immutable: Sirens too might be leggy, as in a superbly camp painting of *Ulysses and the Sirens* by Otto Greiner, showing what looks like a nude boat-race crew sculling past an equally bare trio of lovelies. The Siren, however, always took an active role, whereas the ondine tended to be passive.

Best known of these creatures was the heroine of Friedrich de la Motte Fouqué's 1811 novella *Undine*. In this romance, water-spirit and man fall in love and are married, but the husband then becomes uneasy at the thought that his wife is not of his world. He curses her, at which she disappears

Otto Greiner, *Ulysses and the Sirens* (1902)

into the River Danube, and the husband later marries again, despite a dream warning him that he will lose his life if he does so. Immediately after his second wedding, Undine returns to him, and as she kisses him, he dies. Where he is buried, a stream rises, encircling the grave: 'Even to this day the inhabitants of the village show the spring, and cherish the belief that it is the poor rejected Undine, who in this manner still embraces her husband in her loving arms.' This Undine, then, who takes refuge in a river and reinvents herself as a spring, is a freshwater mermaid rather than a saltwater one. There are differences in how sea-nymphs and river-spirits figure in tradition (see Chapter 8), but for poetic and pictorial purposes, such distinctions were appropriately fluid.

Undine's plot quite precisely follows a passage by the sixteenth-century Swiss-German philosopher Paracelsus:

If a nymph is married to a man, and they happen to be in a boat and he offends her, she will throw herself overboard and disappear. She might as well be dead for him; he never will see

Harold Nelson, *Undine Warns the Knight* (1901)

her again. Yet she is not dead, and he still is wedded to her. He cannot lawfully take another wife, for he is not divorced. He is bound to her for eternity, though she has departed from husband and children. If the man should nevertheless take another wife, the nymph will kill him, which has happened many times.

This in turn echoes the twelfth-century author Gervase of Tilbury, who declares that some men become lovers of demons or fairies, 'and when they have transferred their affections with a view to marrying other women, they have died before they could enjoy carnal union with their new partners.' Gervase says this is 'something we do know, confirmed daily as it is by men who are above all reproach'. Like Paracelsus's assertion that what he describes 'has happened many times', this suggests a very widespread piece of lore.

Paracelsus expanded on the subject in an essay on 'Nymphs, Sylphs, Pygmies, and Salamanders', which he called collectively 'elementals' – beings he believed lived in water, air, earth and fire. These, he wrote, had no souls, but could sometimes acquire them:

Nymphs come to us out of the water, make themselves known and seen, and then return to their elements.

Since the elementals resemble man except in one respect, that they do not possess an immortal soul, it can be understood that if a nymph should appear to a man and he marries her, she can live with him and bear children. These children then are endowed with a soul because one parent is from Adam, and the other [i.e. the nymph] has received the gift of soul and immortality, and become a human being by the sacrament of marriage and union with God and man.

The idea that a non-human creature could be redeemed and given eternal life by marriage with a mortal helped inspire both *Undine* and Andersen's 'Little Mermaid', two tales that put their supernatural heroines in direct relationship with man. Becoming part of the cultural canon, these elementals gained immortality in at least that sense.

Like 'The Little Mermaid', *Undine* was turned into both opera and ballet. Tales of mermaids lend themselves well to musical adaptation, partly because music is an integral part of the legend. Ever since Homer wrote of the Sirens, it has been said that supernatural sea-beings enchanted mortals with their song. Music can convey magic; it can represent the flowing notes of water; it can express love or desire. All these elements come together in the mermaid romance, a challenge and invitation to a composer.

Slavic tales of rusalkas, dangerous nymphs that haunt dark forest pools, inspired several operas. In Dvořák's *Rusalka* (1900), a water-spirit falls in love with a prince and finally, like Undine, kills him with a kiss. An earlier work, Pushkin's drama *Rusalka* (1832), scored by Dargomyzhsky in 1855, follows folk traditions that identify rusalkas as the souls of suicides or unbaptised children. His central character is a peasant girl left pregnant by a faithless lover, who drowns herself and then becomes empress of an underwater kingdom.

Debussy's *Pelléas et Mélisande* (1902), with a libretto from Maurice Maeterlinck's play of 1893, tells of a mysterious woman who meets a prince by a woodland stream, marries him, then falls in love with his brother, and finally dies in childbirth. Her watery nature is a recurrent theme: she loses her crown in the river and her wedding ring in a fountain, and both her flowing tears and her long flowing hair are key elements in the text, which is obliquely based on the medieval

Mikhail Vrubel, *Rusalka* (1891)

French legend of Mélusine (see Chapter 9).

Germany, meanwhile, has the Rhine Maidens. Richard Wagner's Ring Cycle (1848–74) begins, in *Rhinegold*, with a scene in which three River Daughters have their golden treasure stolen by the dwarf Alberich, a theft leading to a curse that eventually destroys the gods themselves. The fourth and final work, *Götterdämmerung* ('The Twilight of the Gods'), ends when the Maidens seize back the Ring that has been made from their gold, just before Valhalla, home of the gods, is seen burning.

The Maidens have no direct equivalent in Germanic legend, unlike the rest of the Ring Cycle's characters, but a medieval work from which many of those characters are drawn, the Norse *Saga of Thidrek*, features a mermaid with significant connections. King Vilkinus of Sweden was

ieweile hatte Hagen
Den Schatz viel gar genommen,
Eh' der reiche König
Wieder war gekommen;
Er senkte ihn zu Loche
Allen in den Rhein.
Er wähnte sein zu genießen;
Das sollt' ihm nicht beschieden seyn.

Die Fürsten kamen wieder,
Mit ihnen viele Mannen;
Kriemhild mit Frauen und Mägden
Zu klagen da begannen
Ihren großen Schaden;
Ihnen war bitter leid.
Gerne wär' Giselher
Zu allen Treuen ihr bereit.

Da sprachen sie in Gleichem:
„Er hat viel übel gethan."
Er entwich der Fürsten Zorne,
Bis wieder er gewann

Julius Schnorr von Carolsfeld and Eugen Neureuther,
woodcut illustration from *Der Nibelungen Noth* (1843)

travelling with his army along the shores of the Baltic when he met a woman:

> She was fair, and he set his mind on her and lay with her. This was none other than the woman known as a mermaid, who had the nature that she was a monster in the sea but seemed to be a woman on land.

After seducing the mermaid, the king went on his way, but when he was back on board his ship and had put out to sea, she rose from the water and took the vessel by the stern, holding it motionless. Vilkinus promised that if she cared to come to his own country, he would treat her well, so she released the ship and swam along behind it to Sweden. Here, after several months had passed, she told Vilkinus that she was carrying his child. Having given birth to a boy, she departed from the king's life and from the story.

Her son Vadi, however, grew up to be a giant, and *his* son, Voelund or Vaulundr, became a significant figure in Scandinavian and Teutonic myth. (Both Vadi and Voelund were also known in British legend, under the anglicised names Wade and Wayland.) The Norse sagas tell us that as a boy, Voelund was apprenticed to the craftsman Mime – who in Wagner's mythology is the forger of the fatal Ring, and brother of Alberich, who stole the Rhine Maidens' gold.

Both the *Saga of Thidrek* and another of Wagner's sources, the thirteenth-century German poem the *Nibelungenlied*, mention two female water-spirits who predict that the heroes will meet disaster (a warning that is ignored). In *Thidrek*, the warriors encounter the nymphs by the Danube where it flows together with the Rhine – a fictional piece of geography, but one that has resonance in the context of the Rhine Maidens.

Postcard showing a sailor lured to destruction by Lorelei
(Ottmar Zieher, Munich, 1904)

Apart from associations with the right river, however, these prophetic beings seem not much more relevant than Voelund's mermaid grandmother when considered as Wagnerian prototypes, and in fact Wagner was probably influenced more directly by a visual source than by any story. He owned an 1843 edition of the *Nibelungenlied* with magnificent woodcuts, one of which imaginatively interprets the depositing of a great treasure in the Rhine. In the illustration – entirely without support from the text, which simply tells how the gold and jewels were hidden in the river – three mermaids wait in the depths to receive the loot. Here, it appears, is the inspiration for the Rhine Maidens, unknown in the medieval sagas but strikingly displayed in this nineteenth-century picture.

In folklore, treasure-guarding is a function more usually attributed to dragons or serpents than to mermaids, and indeed later in Wagner's Cycle a dragon appears, from whom in turn the Ring is taken. Mermaids and dragons, however, are more closely related than one might suppose: the scaly tail of certain supernatural women, such as Mélusine, is described as that of a snake rather than a fish, and in Elizabethan poetry a mermaid can be classed as a serpent, while both dragons and serpents are 'worms' in medieval English. Among the attributes of the Rhine Daughters there is a reptilian hoarding tendency, although they also share the traditional mermaid propensity to lure and drown men.

Unrelated to Wagner's Maidens but closely linked to the same river is another musical nymph. In the early seventeenth century it was said that the Lurley or Lorle rock formation above the Rhine was haunted. From the mid eighteenth century, the rock's previously non-specific spirit became gendered as female, and in a ballad of 1802 by Clemens Brentano she was given a history as a fisherman's daughter seduced, abandoned, and then transformed into the sorceress Lore Lay – thus turning a landscape feature into a legend. Heinrich Heine's poem *Die Lorelei* (1823) tells how the lady, with her wondrous beauty and enchanting song, entices a sailor to his doom, and the folkish melody woven around Heine's words by Friedrich Silcher in 1837 attained the status of unofficial national anthem, sung by homesick Germans everywhere.

It's significant that, like the heroine of Pushkin's *Rusalka*, Lorelei is given a back-story explaining her supernatural powers in terms of her betrayal by a lover, or in other words her erotic experience, however innocently acquired. In music as in art, the mermaid's character is often determined by her sexuality and her relationship with men.

Three

MERMAID WIVES AND
OTHER FOLKLORE

The nineteenth-century population explosion of mermaids in music, painting and literature arose partly from a new interest in folklore. Early in the century, scholars in Germany, Scotland and Ireland started collecting traditional tales and ballads that had been passed on in rural communities by word of mouth, often over generations. Transcribed and published, sometimes in revised and embellished versions, those tales soon reached an international readership, inspiring researchers in other countries to record their own native legends, and providing a rich fund of material in plot and imagery for creative artists.

Certain folktales, as became apparent from comparisons between the national collections, were similar across continents: one story found almost worldwide, in various versions, tells of a man taking a water-spirit for a wife. In Ireland, it remained a standard tale throughout the twentieth century, as in this example recorded in 1937:

As a man was walking along the strand of Glenbeigh, he saw a mermaid sitting on a rock combing her hair. He stole over to where she was and seeing a little cap near her he took it, and the mermaid, looking around for her cap, could not find it. By losing this cap she had also lost her power to return to the sea.

The man then brought her home and married her. They lived happily together with their children for a long time until one day the man was cleaning the loft in which he kept his fishing tackle, and he threw down the mermaid's cap. The minute she saw it she grabbed at it and off with her back to the sea.

Her husband and children were all very lonely after her.

Plenty of far more elaborate versions have been told and written down. This is what's called a 'migratory legend', a tale told in different places, often with local detail making it specific to the teller's neighbourhood – as in the reference above to Glenbeigh strand, a beach in County Kerry – but always the same in essentials. First, the man sees the mermaid, and steals her magic cap (or belt, or cloak, or even tail, understood in such cases as something that can be taken off like a skirt). Then the mermaid marries the man, having little choice in the matter, and bears his children. Finally, the mermaid finds her enchanted garment, and returns to the water.

Certain variants are characteristic of certain regions. In Ireland, the Hebrides and the islands of Shetland and Orkney, the magic garment is often a sealskin, and the water-woman is a selkie, one of the seal-people (see Chapter 4). In Germany, the otherworldly bride may be a swan-maiden, with a feather cloak; in Polynesia, she takes the form of a porpoise; in China, a water-dragon or serpent. In all cases, though, the essential point is the wife's dual nature. She may appear at times as a woman and at others as a water-creature (seal, swan), or she may be half-and-half like a traditional mermaid, or she may look like a woman always, but be able to live in the sea when she's wearing

'The Peasant and the Mermaid', illustration to Fletcher Bassett's
Legends and Superstitions of the Sea (1885)

her magic cap – whichever way she's described, she is both human *and* animal.

Unlike the Little Mermaid, she always has legs, though they may be hidden by her tail or animal skin, and the loss of her garment is physically painless. Emotionally, though, it's another matter. Some narrators say in so many words that the mermaid's miserable on land, but they hardly have to spell it out: when she finds her talisman, she invariably heads straight back to the sea, her true element. Sometimes she's sad to leave her children, and sometimes she takes them with her. Sometimes she has a first husband waiting in the water, and sometimes another set of children there too. Sometimes she visits her land family, bringing them gifts of fish – but never, in folktales, does she elect to stay on shore.

The wife's experience, exiled from her element, confined in an alien relationship, presents a psychological symbol that has been explored by dramatists and poets. Ibsen's play *The Lady from the Sea* (1888) steers just clear of the explicitly supernatural, but makes his heroine Ellida's position plain by repeatedly comparing her to a mermaid trapped in the shallows, dying because she can neither live on land nor escape to deep water. Devoted to her husband, but unable to forget her first lover, a sailor she says was 'like the sea', Ellida is torn between social stability and primal wildness. Finally her husband offers her liberty of choice, a freedom that resolves her dilemma and enables her to stay with him, so that unusually (both for Ibsen and in terms of the legend) the play ends with her contented adjustment to society.

Seamus Heaney's poem 'Maighdean Mara' ('Sea Maiden'), published in a collection of 1972, is based on the usual story:

> He stole her garments as
> She combed her hair: follow
> Was all that she could do.
> He hid it in the eaves
> And charmed her there, four walls,
> Warm floor, man-love nightly
> In earshot of the waves.

His structure, however, suggests a realistically tragic conclusion, beginning and ending with the lines:

> She sleeps now, her cold breasts
> Dandled by undertow.

Heaney has said he was writing partly about a neighbour's wife who drowned herself, and that for him, the legend's central theme is of someone 'trapped into a domestic life by a mistake'.

The reverse image of sea-wife as captive is mermaid as active wooer, enticing the man she has her eye on to join her in the

Edvard Munch, *The Lady from the Sea* (1896)

waves. 'The Wonderful Tune', a tale from Thomas Crofton Croker's *Fairy Legends and Traditions of the South of Ireland* (1828), begins with a piper called Maurice Connor playing music by the seashore. One jig he knew was so lively that even the fish danced, and after a while a mermaid came to join them. She asked Maurice to marry her, a proposal that horrified his mother: 'Oh then, as if I was not widow enough before, there he is going away from me to be married to that scaly woman,' she cried. Ignoring her protests, Maurice swam off with his sea-nymph, and was never seen again on land, though sailors around the Kerry coast said they often heard the sound of his pipes from underwater.

Several Victorian and Edwardian writers used the irresistible mermaid either as character or metaphor, or as both together. In H.G. Wells's novella *The Sea Lady* (1902), 'a properly constituted mermaid with a real physical tail' is brought to shore in Folkestone. Her charm is too strong for a promising young politician, who finally abandons his career, his human fiancée, and indeed his life, when he takes to the sea with his aquatic beloved and is tenderly drowned by her.

More straightforwardly comic, but still a story of a drowning, is the popular eighteenth-century song 'Married to a Mermaid', written to the tune of 'Rule, Britannia':

> Oh! 'twas on the deep Atlantic,
> In the equinoctial gales,
> That a young feller fell overboard,
> Among the sharks and whales;
> He fell right down so quickly,
> So headlong down fell he,
> That he went out of sight like a streak of light,
> To the bottom of the deep blue sea,
> Singing Rule, Britannia, Britannia rules the waves,
> Britons never, never, never shall be slaves.

Far below, he meets a mermaid:

> She raised herself on her beautiful tail,
> And gave him her wet white hand.
> Saying, 'Long have I waited for you, my dear,
> You're welcome safe to land.
> Go back to your messmates for the last time,
> And tell them all from me,
> That you're ma-ri-ed to a mer-mi-ed,
> At the bottom of the deep blue sea.'

Bidding him a final farewell, his captain shouts over the side:

> 'Be as happy as you can with your wife, my man,
> There's no Divorce Court at the bottom of the sea.'

In European tradition, then, there are two basic types of water-bride, those who are kept on land and domesticated

Songsheet cover for 'Married to a Mermaid' (*c.*1866)

for a while, but finally make their escape back to the waves, and others who entice their husbands into the sea, from which there is no return.

West African legend features a different kind of mermaid-wife. Mami Wata, or Mammy Water, is a fishtailed goddess said to marry human husbands, who then come under her

Zoumana Sane, *Mami Wata* (*c.*1987)

protection, gaining prestige and wealth. One man supposed to have made this sort of 'water-marriage' was John Stuart-Young, an Englishman who lived in West Africa in the first few decades of the twentieth century. Known to be homosexual, he was socially accepted, according to some accounts, largely because of his presumed association with the mermaid-queen: marriage with a mermaid excuses a man from taking a human bride.

Stuart-Young's union with Mami Wata was a matter of rumour. In contrast, a first-person report appeared in *Lagos Weekend* in 1987, by a man calling himself 'Tony White' – apparently a typical pseudonym in Nigerian tabloids, and one that has extra resonance here, since Mami Wata is said to be pale skinned, her image a blend of European folktales spread by slave traders, and indigenous African legends of water-spirits. Tony wrote that after a sexual encounter with a beautiful girl, he had been transported to an underwater realm where he met Mami Wata, who told him that since he belonged to her line of descent, he should pay her special attention. Waking, he found Mami's ring on his finger, and from that time renounced his former life of sensual pleasure, devoting himself to the worship of his ancestress/wife and making regular sacrifices to her.

This is a possibly unique case of someone claiming to have married a mermaid *himself*. Generally, such tales are told in the third person, in the past and/or in some other place, distancing the fabulous event from the teller's present reality.

While legends of recent times tend to focus on the mermaid's intimate relationships with men, traditionally just as important was a more general and elemental association with the sea. At least until the nineteenth century, it was common lore among sailors that to see a mermaid was a bad omen, since her appearance inevitably portended a storm.

That belief is central to a ballad widely known in both Britain and America in various versions, generally called 'The Mermaid':

On Friday morning as we set sail
It was not far from land
O there we espied a fair pretty maid
With the comb and a glass in hand, her hand, her hand
With the comb and glass in hand.

O the stormy winds they did blow
And the raging seas they did roar
While we poor sailor boys go up aloft
And the landlubbers lie down below, below, below
And the landlubbers lie down below.

A cabin-boy grieves for his parents, soon to be bereaved, and a sailor for his wife. The captain declares that all on board will drown, and the final verse could be spoken by any one of the crew:

The moon shone bright and the stars gave light
And my mother is looking for me
She may look, she may weep, O with watery eyes
That I lie at the bottom of the sea.

The mermaid here does not, it seems, deliberately set out to provoke disaster: her mere presence is enough to raise the stormy winds, and the same idea is implicit in both Andersen's and Disney's versions of 'The Little Mermaid', whose heroines have only to look at the craft bearing their loved prince for a tempest to blow.

Often, however, it was believed that mermaids not only could bring on a storm, but did so with malice. In Shakespeare's *Henry VI Part 3*, the Duke of Gloucester declares, 'Why, I can smile, and murder while I smile . . . I'll drown more sailors than the mermaid shall' (Act III Scene 2), a reference implying

Bicci di Lorenzo, *St Nicholas of Bari Rebuking the Storm* (1433–5)

that like the villainous Duke – later Richard III – the mermaid knew just what she was doing.

A fifteenth-century painting by Bicci di Lorenzo, *St Nicholas of Bari Rebuking the Storm*, shows the saint hovering above a ship to calm the winds, while at bottom left of the picture, a tiny mermaid flees the holy presence. Her marginal appearance would have been understood by contemporary viewers as signifying not only an evil pagan influence cast out by the power of God, but the original reason for the ship's peril.

A more rationalising position was taken in the seventeenth century by the clergyman John Swan, who argued in his *Speculum Mundi* that 'Mermaids and Men-fish' – whose existence he accepted without question – had no power to change the weather. Instead, their animal instincts made them more sensitive than humans to atmospheric conditions, so that they made a 'whooping noise' before a gale: in other words, they could *predict* rather than *initiate* a tempest.

An ability to prophesy is often ascribed to fairy beings, whose supernatural qualities can include a transcendence of human time that enables them to see past and future, or even association with 'fate' itself, a word etymologically linked with 'fairy' and 'fay'. Mermaids, who on one analysis are water-fairies, can share this skill. Benjamin Thorpe reports in his *Northern Mythology* (1852) that in Norway, merchildren, called Marmæler, 'are sometimes caught by fishermen, who take them home, that they may gain from them a knowledge of future events; for both they, as well as the Mermen and Mermaids, can see into futurity'.

The oracular talents of Scandinavian mermaids were reported a good deal earlier. Erich Pontoppidan, Bishop of Bergen, wrote in the 1750s of 'a Mer-maid, that called herself Isbrandt, and held several conversations with a peasant at Samsoe; in which she foretold the birth of

John Flaxman, *Ulysses and the Sirens* from *The Odyssey* (1793)

Christian IV. and made the peasant preach repentance to the courtiers, who were very much given to drunkenness'. Pontoppidan, incidentally, cites this story only as an example of an idle fable: although he firmly believed in the existence of mermaid-like animals, he was equally certain that they could neither speak, sing, nor predict.

In the sixteenth century, Paracelsus wrote of the elementals that some of them 'know the past, present and future of humanity'. Going back to the medieval *Nibelungenlied* that inspired Wagner, we read that when the warrior Hagen met two river-maidens:

> They floated on the waves before him like water-fowl, and this led him to think that they were gifted with second sight, so that he more readily believed whatever they told him. And indeed they told him all that he wished to know of them.

The gift of foresight or farsightedness, common to many water-spirits, can be traced all the way back to Homer and the Sirens Odysseus encounters, who invite him to share their supernatural knowledge. In Pope's translation, they tempt the hero:

> Approach; thy soul shall into raptures rise;
> Approach, and learn new wisdom from the wise.
> We know whate'er the kings of mighty name
> Achieved at Ilion in the field of fame;
> Whate'er beneath the sun's bright journey lies.
> Oh stay, and learn new wisdom from the wise.

Four

SELKIES

Similar to mermaids in many respects are selkies, the seal-folk. Tales of them are told mainly in Ireland, Scotland and Scandinavia, places where seals were once abundant, and where seal-hunting was historically an important part of the coastal economy. The fur can be made into coats, the flesh eaten, and the oil used for fuel, making the dead seal a valuable commodity; the living seal's appetite for salmon and other fish, meanwhile, make it the fisherman's enemy, and provide another reason for slaughter.

In many parts of the world, seal-hunts continue, as does the conservation debate, but before any movement got underway for the preservation of seals, legends were common among those who came in close contact with the animals, suggesting that they were powerful and enchanted beings, to be treated with respect.

David Thomson's book *The People of the Sea* (1954), an absorbing account of seal lore current in the mid twentieth century in Scotland and the west of Ireland, makes clear the close relationship between shore dwellers and seals. As one Orkney man said, 'the seals and ourselves were aye thrown together in the way o' getting a living, and everything we feel, they feel, ye may be sure o' that.'

The idea that seals shared human feelings could be extended to the notion that they had human speech. An Irish informant told Thomson of a man called Diarmid ac Eoghain, who shot seals for sport:

Oh, he used to be out every day with his gun shooting them as fast as he met them, until one day he saw a mother seal and a young one along with her. But didn't she speak when he raised his gun! 'Don't, don't, Diarmid ac Eoghain,' said she, 'till I give the breast to my little one.' 'I won't or ever again,' said Diarmid to her. And they say he never shot a seal from that day on.

Another tale focusing specifically on the killing of seals, which Thomson heard in north-east Scotland, dealt with a seal hunter called Angus Ruadh, who was taken under the sea by a stranger, and was there confronted with an old man, injured and on the point of death. This, he was told, was a seal he had stabbed that day – the stranger's father. Only Angus, who had made the wound, could heal it, by closing the cut with his own hand. He did so, and the old seal-man was well again. Angus was made to swear a solemn oath that he would never kill or hurt another seal, and was then taken back to his home on dry land.

Here, the stranger and his father not only speak but look like human beings, and this idea is central to a number of legends where the seals' skins, in which they appear as animals, are a magical device that lets them travel through the sea. When on land, they can take off their furry hides, and are revealed as men and women. These are the selkie folk.

A selkie girl, it's said, is irresistibly beautiful without her sealskin, and any man who sees her will fall passionately in love with her. If he can steal her covering, he has her in his power, since each selkie can wear her own skin and no other. If that's lost, the selkie must stay on land until she finds it again. This is, of course, the same idea as the mermaid's cap or belt, and indeed the fable of a man who marries a sea-bride is classified, according to academic lists of folktale types, as 'The seal woman', the mermaid-wife being considered a variant rather than the original.

In fact, Scandinavian and Teutonic legends of swan-women, who took off their white cloaks to marry mortal men, probably predate tales of the seals' transformations. Returning to Voelund, grandson of King Vilkinus and the mermaid, it's related in the Icelandic poems known as the *Edda*, which date back to the eighth century, that he and his brothers married three Valkyries. These were mythic women who assisted warriors in battle, and in this case they appeared as swans: when wearing their feathered robes, they could fly, and without their disguises they were revealed as beautiful maidens. Stories like this may have helped to inspire selkie legends, which in turn seem to have led to the idea that the mermaid too could shed her aquatic garment. As already noted, what animal made up the mermaid's 'other half', whether bird, seal, fish or reptile, was not always an essential point.

Some theorists, however, have proposed a historically specific basis for tales of selkie brides, relating them to the hide-covered canoes and sealskin coats of the Inuits. In the distant past, so goes the argument, natives of Greenland and the far north of Scandinavia used to cross the sea, fetching up in Shetland, where the women were sometimes captured by the coast-dwellers and kept as wives. Without their furs

'Seal and Mermaid', engraving from John Timbs'
Eccentricities of the Animal Creation (1869)

John D. Batten's illustration to 'The Swan Maidens' from
Joseph Jacobs' *Europa's Fairy Book* (1916): like selkies, swan
princesses can appear in animal or human form

and kayaks, they could not escape: and so we come to legends
of selkies trapped into marriage.

This idea is characteristic of the late nineteenth century,
when it was a fashion to interpret folklore in supposedly
factual terms. Provocative though the notion may be, it
doesn't stand up well to closer scrutiny. As mentioned above,
stories of seals that metamorphose into human shape are
not demonstrably more ancient than those of birds and
other animals doing likewise, and even if we allow that
Shetlanders and Orcadians may have taken Inuit wives who
wore sealskin, we can't suppose, for example, that Germanic
tribes habitually captured women dressed in swan-feathers.

A link with far northern regions, however, does exist. In
old Scandinavian legend, magical powers were attributed to

the Finns, and when Norsemen invaded the Shetlands and Orkneys, they brought their folklore with them. Traditions of Finn-folk, also spelt Fin-folk, a name suggesting the fins of a sea-beast as well as the natives of Finland, remained current in the islands well into the nineteenth century, some tales identifying the Finn-men with the selkies, others portraying them as foreign sorcerers travelling the waves in unsinkable craft. Someone in a kayak – a vessel that stays afloat under almost any circumstances – can look as if they're swimming with their top half out of the water, like a seal, and though we shouldn't try to explain away a whole myth, we may accept an influence.

In mainland Scotland and the Hebrides, as well as in Shetland, it's a feature of certain stories that the selkies are from Scandinavia. At the conclusion of Angus Ruadh's adventure, described above, he is rewarded by the seals with a bag of 'Dane's gold'. A common Scottish tale deals with a fisherman who wounds but does not kill a seal, which then swims off taking the man's knife with it. Some while later, the man visits a house in Norway, where he sees his own knife. 'I was that seal,' the householder tells the fisherman.

In Scandinavia itself, the relationship between men and seal-folk can be a terrible one. A story from William Craigie's *Scandinavian Folklore* (1896), located in Mikladal on the island of Kalsoy in the Faeroes, starts in the usual way, with a fisherman who marries a seal-wife and has several children with her. Inevitably, she leaves him, returning to her first husband in the sea, but some while later she visits her human partner in a dream, when he's about to go seal-hunting in a particular coastal cave. She warns him not to hurt her seal-husband nor her seal-children, and tells him exactly whereabouts in the cave they will be. Ignoring the dream, the man and his friends kill all the seals they can, and he himself takes home the corpse of his wife's mate and the hands and feet of her children. That night, when the men have boiled the head of the big seal and the flippers of the young ones for their dinner, his wife comes in 'like a fearful troll', sniffs at the dishes, and cries a curse on the men of Mikladal, that they should drown at sea and fall off the cliffs until the number of dead is so great that they can encircle the whole of Kalsoy, holding each other by the hand.

Although the legend of the seal-wife is central, there is also much selkie lore dealing with seal-men and their unions with human women. One of the most haunting of ballads, recorded in various versions from the Orkneys and Shetlands between the mid nineteenth and mid twentieth centuries, combines the theme of a seal fathering a human child with that of the seal hunt. It has been given different titles, and is perhaps best known as 'The Great Silkie of Sule Skerry', but the lyrics sent to the folklorist John Campbell of Islay in 1859 are headed simply 'Sealchie Sang' (Selkie Song). While a mother is rocking her baby son's cradle, a 'grimly Ghost' of a seal appears, and announces that he is the child's father. His territory, he tells the woman, is among the rocks of Sule Skerry, a remote reef in the North Atlantic, where he will take his selkie son in a year's time. The mother declares:

My husband is a proud gunner
An aye a proud gunner is he
An' the first shot that he will fire
Will be at my young son an' thee.

Stamps showing selkies, issued in the Faroe Islands (2007)

She is punished for her unmaternal wish, when the gunner misses his aim, and shoots her dead. The seal and his son swim out to sea, mourning for her.

Several families were traditionally said to have a seal among their ancestors. The Connollys or Coneelys of Ireland were rumoured to have seal-blood, and so were the MacCodrums of Uist in the Western Isles of Scotland. The latter were widely known as the Clan MacCodrum of the Seal, and none of them, according to more than one account, would ever kill one of the animals. Most famous of the family (apart from the progenitive seal) was the eighteenth-century poet John MacCodrum, who wrote a Gaelic verse to what is described as 'one of the old North Uist seal songs'. That could mean a tune played by seal hunters, but MacCodrum's words are sung in the person of the seal, lamenting the death of its kin at men's hands.

Both seals and selkies are associated with music. Naturalists have noted that seals are responsive auditors, more sensitive than humans to pitch, and able to distinguish the cries of their own babies from hundreds of others. Captain William Scoresby, explorer of the Arctic, wrote in 1820 that a tune, particularly the sound of someone whistling, would draw a seal to the surface of the waves.

Legend has it that a selkie woman returning to the sea will sing in rapture, an idea that may be inspired by more than pure fantasy. In *A Life of Song* (1929), the musicologist Marjory Kennedy-Fraser reports a remarkable experience she had on the island of Barra, in the Western Isles of Scotland, while sunbathing with two other musicians and watching grey seals basking on the rocks. One of her friends suggested she sang a tune she had noted down from an old Hebridean woman who called it a seal song. When she sang the first phrase:

> Instantly there was a response from the seal rocks. Like a fusillade, single note after single note came from each seal in succession from the southerly end of the reefs to the north.
>
> Then, from out a few seconds of intense silence, came a beautiful solo voice which sang to us a phrase we had never heard before. . . . The voice of the seal was so beautiful (of a rich mezzo-soprano quality) and the *cantabile* so perfect, that I should almost have believed I had been dreaming but for the corroboration of my two musician fellow-hearers.

When Kennedy-Fraser told this story in London, she was hardly credited. *Punch*, she notes, suggested that 'the British National Opera might retrieve its losses by capturing and

Paul Balluriau, *Sirens* (*c.*1895)

exploiting that same seal prima donna!'

Seal song, however, is a phenomenon that has been reliably reported, and recordings have been made of seals vocalising both underwater and on land. The seal is, by nature, much of what the mermaid is by legend: a streamlined, graceful swimmer; a creature that can come on land but prefers her own element; the object of man's admiration and the victim of his rapacity. She also, like a Siren, sings.

Five

ZOOLOGICAL MERMAIDS

It's been proposed that a mermaid is just a seal; that people long ago mistook seals for fishtailed women underwater, and that all of the rest of a mermaid's attributes are fictions pinned to the hide of a real animal. That kind of reductionist argument shrinks a myth to a misidentification, but it's worth considering the questions around what we might call the zoological mermaid, as opposed to the legendary being.

How do we know that mermaids *don't* exist? If we discount the more obviously fantastic features such as comb and mirror, and a wish or willingness to enter matrimony, what's left is the persuasive idea that the sea contains more than we know, and in some remote part of it might live something that looks like a human with a fishtail.

One counter-argument is that a creature so vulnerable to attack, without sharp teeth or other defence, could only survive by swimming in large shoals, which would have been reliably documented by now. Geneticists, meanwhile, state that to exist as imagined, with a true woman's body and fish's tail, a mermaid would contradict the laws of evolution, since fish and humans come from branches of the phylogenetic tree that separated hundreds of millions of years ago.

In 2012, images of a 'mermaid skeleton' circulated
on social media, created by digital manipulation

Neither submission, probably, would convince a thorough-going believer in mermaids. A mermaid has arms and hands, giving her a certain advantage over even a shark; and as for evolution, can we be certain that fossils might not one day be found of a long-vanished ancestor bridging the gap between land and marine primates?

Advocates maintain even now that mermaids could be, and are. One recent set of sightings, from 2009, comes from Kiryat Yam in Israel, where a girl with a tail was said to appear at sunset, lying on the sand or swimming in the sea. This might have been a dugong, an animal often mentioned

Mermaid meets manatee, late nineteenth-century engraving

in connection with the mermaid legend, together with its relative the manatee. They belong to an order known as Sirenians, named after the Siren of mythology, showing how closely they have been associated with fabulous mermaids. Manatees can live in fresh or salt water, and survive today in the Amazon and around West Africa, as well as in Florida; dugongs live in salt water only, and can be found from Australia and the Indian Ocean to the Red Sea, including the coast of Israel.

Like seals, dugongs and manatees have been claimed to be the foundation of the mermaid myth, and, again like seals, they have their own legends in their own habitats, stories that resemble those of the European mermaid. Their looks, however, are hardly aphrodisiac. They have huge lips with bristly whiskers, tiny eyes on the sides of the head, and no neck to speak of. While it might require enchantment or at least mental agility to fall in love with a seal, surely only a Sirenian could fancy another Sirenian – although Elaine Morgan notes in her *Descent of Woman* (1972) that:

> in the Red Sea area there is an oral tradition that in former centuries a sailor after months at sea who found a dugong in the shallows – large, docile, warm-blooded, air-breathing, smooth-skinned, female breasted, and with ventral [frontal] genital organs which remarkably well fitted his own – wouldn't worry overmuch if she was comparatively faceless.

If the tradition is true, such a sailor of all people would have been able to attest that what he had mated with was wholly animal.

From a distance, however, and to someone who already had a mental image of mermaids, the sight of a dugong raising its upper body from the waves, or flipping up its tail, could suggest that here was the original. Christopher Columbus recorded in his journal for January 1493 that when exploring the Rio Yaque del Norte in what is now the Dominican Republic, a place where dugongs still live, he saw three *serenas* (mermaids), who rose high out of the water. He noted that these Sirens 'were not so fair as they are painted'.

Another candidate for the role of mermaid-lookalike is the walrus. The explorer William Scoresby wrote in 1820:

> It is not at all improbable that the walrus has afforded foundation for some of the stories of mermaids. I have myself seen a sea-horse [walrus] in such a position, that it requires little stretch of imagination to mistake it for a human being; so like, indeed, was it, that the surgeon of the ship actually reported to me that he had seen a man with his head just appearing above the surface of the water.

Traditions of mermaids as semi-human or semi-divine can be distinguished from belief in them as animals pure and simple, beasts that may be rare but can be observed and even caught. Sightings are still reported: the 2009 example from Israel is one of several to be found on the Internet. Many similar accounts appeared in the twentieth-century press, some provoking considerable argument, as correspondents put their cases for the existence or non-existence of mermaids.

Going back to the early nineteenth century, we find a positive epidemic of observations, close encounters, and actual captures, many occurring around the shores of Scotland, Ireland and Wales. It's probably no coincidence that this was also the period when Celtic folktales about mermaids became widely read and repeated. Some of the personal accounts, to a sceptical mind, are clearly embroidered or illusory, going into detail about blue eyes, rosy cheeks, shapely shoulders and so forth, but a significant number describe creatures with monkey faces, stark white or greyish skin, and vestigial upper limbs. You could not marry them, nor want to, but they might be real if unusual fish or aquatic mammals.

Taking just one of numerous examples, in 1823, some Shetland fishermen found a beast about three foot long entangled in their nets, with breasts like a woman but a dogfish's tail. It had a bristly crest on its head, and hairless skin, and made 'a low plaintive sound' when the men took it into their boat. After a couple of hours they released it, but they later reported their catch to a zoologist, who recorded that of the six men involved, 'not one. . . dreams of a doubt of its being a Mermaid'. To these fishermen, it seems clear, a mermaid was not a legendary being of otherworldly beauty, but simply an odd-looking animal.

In the eighteenth century, there was comparatively little discussion of mermaids, although Erich Pontoppidan wrote about them at some length in his *Natural History of Norway* (published in Danish in 1751). While dismissing accounts of creatures who sang or prophesied, he did not doubt the reality of sea-animals somewhat resembling humans. He had, he said, interviewed many eye-witnesses from around Bergen and elsewhere, who all agreed that they had seen such beasts in the water.

In a 1717 illustrated guide to the fish and crustaceans of the Moluccas (the Maluku Islands of Indonesia) there is a picture of a 'monster resembling a Siren' that was caught and kept in a barrel for four days, after which, having refused food, it died. Around three foot long, and thin like an eel, it is depicted with breasts and a human face. Modern naturalists have suggested that it was a young dugong, although the drawing doesn't look much like one.

'Mermaid and fishes of Amboyna', engraving based on illustration from Louis Renard, *Poissons des Isles Moluques* (1717)

Earlier again, several accounts came from travellers in hitherto uncharted seas and rivers. Writing about his explorations of Newfoundland in 1610, Captain Richard Whitbourne mentioned 'a strange Creature' seen in St Johns:

> which very swiftly came swimming towards mee, looking cheerfully on my face, as it had been a woman: by the face, eyes, nose, mouth, chin, eares, necke, and forehead, it seemed to bee so beautifull, and in those parts so well proportioned, having round about the head many blue streakes, resembling haire, but certainly it was no haire. . .

He did not see whether it had breasts. Its back appeared white and smooth, and below the waist, it tapered off into a pointed shape. 'This (I suppose) was a Maremaid, or Mareman.'

The comment about hair, or lack of it, is interesting. Several mermaid-spotters make a point of saying that what they saw did *not* have hair like a classic sea-nymph. The Shetland catch of 1823, for instance, had bristles, while a tailed creature observed near Milford Haven in Wales in the 1780s, although in most respects presenting a very human appearance from the waist upwards, had on its forehead a substance that 'did not at all resemble hair, but was thin, flat, and compact, not much unlike a ribbon'. A mermaid's hair is such an important part of her legend that by emphasising its absence, such reports plainly position themselves on the zoological rather than mythological side of the fence.

Certainly some people took a very practical view of mermaids: a monk who travelled to the Congo in 1632 said they tasted like veal. He was probably eating manatee.

Just as the rhinoceros was sometimes called a unicorn by early European explorers, although all it had in common with the fabulous beast was its single horn, so manatees, dugongs and perhaps other aquatic animals or fish were referred to as mermaids by people who had no other name for them. Whether treated as food or as rare fauna to be described and drawn by natural historians, they were not the same as the mystic being that emerged from the sea to marry humans.

Of course the two sorts of mermaid do overlap and interlock. The common belief among seafarers that to see a mermaid presaged bad weather does not necessarily mean that the sailors thought the mermaid was something outside nature, since some indisputably real birds (storm petrels, for example) were thought to be similarly ominous. Superstitions like this, however, create a grey area between the zoological and the legendary, and when we come to look at dead mermaids displayed as fairground attractions, we see again a confusion between the real and the fabulous.

Six

RED HERRINGS

In my boyhood I well recollect being highly excited by the arrival in our town, at fair-time, of a 'show,' which professed to exhibit a mermaid, whose portrait, on canvas hung outside, was radiant in feminine loveliness and piscine scaliness. I fondly expected to see the very counterpart within, how disposed I did not venture to imagine, but alive and fascinating, of course. Had I not seen her picture? I joyfully paid my coppers, but oh! woful disappointment! I dimly saw, within a dusty glass case, in a dark corner, a shrivelled and blackened little thing which might have been moulded in mud for aught I could see, but which was labelled, 'MERMAID!'

The lower body and tail of a large salmon-like fish had been attached to a monkey's upper body and head so skilfully that the join could hardly be detected. This synthetic wonder, which the naturalist Philip Gosse saw in the 1820s, was typical of its time. In the early nineteenth century, many showmen put preserved or mummified mermaids on display, generally half-monkey and half-fish.

Most of these were made in Japan, where one enterprising fisherman invented a history for his creation. He had caught it alive, he said, and before it died, it had prophesied a period of general good fortune followed by a terrible epidemic. The only cure for the coming disease (according to the mermaid, as reported by the fisherman) would be a picture of the mermaid herself: fortunately, the fisherman had plenty of portraits for sale. Mermaids were not uncommonly thought able to predict future events (see Chapter 3), but the Japanese fisherman had come up with a particularly brilliant bit of marketing.

Without resorting to prophecies, the showmen of eighteenth- and early nineteenth-century Europe and America made good money from their mermaids. Some spectators, like the young Gosse, were rudely surprised by the hideous relics on display, but many more seem to have flocked to the show while quite aware that they were about to see something rather grotesque.

One notorious example was acquired by an American sailor, Captain Eades, in Batavia (now Jakarta). It was said to have been caught by a fisherman in the north of China, who sold it for a small sum, but by the time Eades bought it, the price had increased to 5,000 Spanish dollars, and Eades was later offered double to sell it on, but refused. Reports may have inflated the figures to stimulate interest in the mermaid, which Eades exhibited in Cape Town in 1822, and afterwards in London. It attracted much interest, and heated correspondence in the *Gentleman's Magazine*, some spectators claiming that they could see the join and even the stitches between the mammalian upper body and the fish's tail, others equally convinced that the creature was presented just as it had lived.

From detailed descriptions and engravings in several sources, it is clear this animal was no beauty. It had thin black hair on the head, lips and chin, it was scaly all over, and it bore 'the appearance of having died in great agony', its neck stretched backward and its face contorted. It was about three foot long, with breasts and arms, and a tail like that of a salmon.

Captain Eades's mermaid, later displayed by
P.T. Barnum as a rarity from Fiji

Eades's mermaid could even have been the same that Gosse saw, but then one artificial mermaid was probably much like another, at least of this variety made from a monkey uncomfortably united to a fish.

Another sort of fake was made from a large ray, a flat fish with a long tail and winglike lateral fins which, when the fish is dead, can be folded into odd shapes and dried. One of these was displayed as an 'angel-fish' at a Folkestone fair in the mid nineteenth century, and was described by the naturalist Frank Buckland as having the body of a young girl and the feet and legs of a goose, the rest of the body being like that of a fish.

An article written in 1928 by the ichthyologist Gilbert Whitley explained how a creature like this was constructed. You curl the ray's side fins over its back, and twist its tail into whatever position you like, tying a piece of string round the head to form a neck. When dried in the sun, the flesh shrinks and the jaws project to form a snout, while a prominent arch of cartilage looks like a pair of folded arms, and the nostrils come to resemble eyes, the real eyes being hidden by the curled fins.

Such creations are known as 'Jenny Hanivers', a term

whose etymology has not been established: it seems to have made its first printed appearance in Whitley's article. 'Haniver' might be derived from Anvers, the French name for Antwerp, a place where the hybrids could have been produced; or it might be a corruption of 'Hanover'. A 'Hanover Jack' was nineteenth-century slang for a counterfeit coin, and a 'Hanover Jenny' or 'Jenny Hanover' might be analogous, 'Jenny' meaning 'female', as in 'Jenny Wren'.

Although they were actually fish, sculpted rays were more often supposed to represent dragons than sea-nymphs. More significant as mermaids were the monkey-fish monstrosities that remained a great attraction in museums and fairgrounds throughout the nineteenth century. One was acquired in the 1840s by the great showman Phineas T. Barnum, who displayed it as a 'Feejee mermaid' at the American Museum in New York, where its appearance apparently tripled the profits. Newspapers reported that it appeared to have 'died in

Tampa Bay Times, 13th March 2008: even in the twenty-first century, hoax creations have made the headlines.

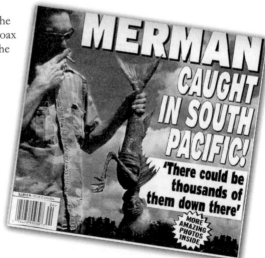

A flyer advertising Barnum's star attraction

great agony', a phrase also used of Captain Eades's treasure, and in fact it seems to have been the same specimen, though the preservation process probably contracted the features of all such creations into unsightly grimaces.

Some spectators wrote letters debunking the supposed marvel, but that may even have encouraged others to go and see it with their own eyes. Barnum himself believed that all publicity was valuable. In a lecture on 'Humbug', he defined the term as 'the art of attracting attention, whether the article is good or bad', and according, again, to Frank Buckland:

> He had an elaborate and really beautiful picture painted, which he hung outside the museum; the picture represented three lovely creatures with beautiful long hair, the traditional looking-glass

and comb, &c. disporting themselves in a fairy-like submarine grotto; but he did *not say* his mermaid was like those in the picture. Attracted by the picture and notice, 'A mermaid is added to the museum, – *No extra charge,*' thousands paid to go in. . .

They then saw a hideous, shrivelled mummy. There is a certain post-modern flavour to all this controversy: viewers were not necessarily expected to *believe* in the reality of mermaids, but paid down their cash all the same, just to see how grossly they were being taken in.

Things had not always been thus. Some eighteenth-century notices of mermaids on display feature drawings of very comely nymphs. In the *Gentleman's Magazine* of 1775 there appears 'an exact drawing of a Syren or Mermaid, now exhibiting in London', whose accompanying description notes her fine blue eyes, small handsome nose, rounded lips and general 'features and complexion of an European'. This creature was 'said to have an enchanting voice, which it never exerts except before a storm'. She had breasts but no nipples, and a belly but no navel (evidently the writer was aware of biological problems inherent in a mammal/fish hybrid). Instead of hair, she had 'a beautiful membrane or fin' on her head – here again, a distinction is made between real hair and the appearance of hair – although the accompanying picture shows a charming belle with what looks like an eighteenth-century coiffure. In the drawing, too, she has both nipples and navel: pictures don't always accurately represent their accompanying descriptions, conventions of traditional mermaids perhaps being stronger in art than in words.

Well into the twentieth century, two hotels in Aden, Yemen, advertised 'Mermaids on Display Here'. The mermaids in

Mermaid in a tank, detail from c.1900 circus poster

question were stuffed dugongs, but at least one writer was inspired to imagine more. In 'Mrs Jorkens', a 1931 story by the fantasy author Lord Dunsany, a man visits an Aden hotel and sees a real, live mermaid sitting in a tank. He falls in love with her, steals her, and marries her; but ultimately, despite the romantic promise of her ocean-deep eyes, she is a boring bourgeoise interested in nothing but local gossip. Jorkens plans to return her to the hotel proprietors, but like other mermaid wives she escapes back to the sea, lobbing her wedding ring at a passing shark.

Live nymphs were indeed sometimes displayed. In 1759, a small mermaid (two foot long) shown at a Paris fair was reported as 'very active, sporting about in the vessel of water in which it was kept with great seeming delight and agility'. This must have been some kind of sea-beast, but larger mermaids might be people dressed up, a practice still followed in the twenty-first century at the Weeki Wachee 'City of Mermaids' in Florida, where swimmers wearing

Weeki Wachee 'City of Mermaids' in Florida (1967)

tails perform in a glass-sided 'theatre', demonstrating their amphibian skill by dancing, eating bananas and drinking soda pop underwater.

Such impersonations were not always for profit. In the 1820s, Robert Hawker, later the vicar of Morwenstow, Cornwall, but then a student, put on a seaweed wig and an oilskin tail and sat for several nights on a seaside rock, loudly singing. When he had attracted enough attention, he made the hoax plain by his finale, a rendition of 'God Save the King', and then dived into the sea. Like many other mermaids, he was a fish that got away.

Seven

THE MERMAID'S SOUL

Returning from manmade and zoological specimens to the legendary mermaid, a question often raised was whether such a creature had a soul. Half-human and half-animal, which half took primacy? Was she a woman with a fish's tail, or a fish with a woman's head and breasts? Could she go to heaven like a human, was she merely a beast without an imperishable spirit, or was she in fact a kind of devil?

The motive force of Disney's Ariel is love: that's the nearest a modern secular interpretation gets to immortal longings. The original Little Mermaid, however, is impelled chiefly by her desire for a blessed eternity, and that's an idea Andersen could have picked up not just from Paracelsus, but from a number of folktales current in his native Denmark.

The Nökke or Neck, a spirit of Danish and Swedish rivers, was said to be concerned about its afterlife. In a legend from Thomas Keightley's *Fairy Mythology* (1850):

Two boys were one time playing near a river that ran by their father's house. The Neck rose and sat on the surface of the water, and played on his harp; but one of the children said to him, 'What is the use, Neck, of your sitting there and playing? you will never be saved.' The Neck then began to weep bitterly, flung away his harp, and sank down to the bottom. The children went home, and told the whole story to their father, who was the parish priest. He said they were wrong to say so to the Neck, and desired them to go immediately back to the river, and console him with the promise of salvation. They did so; and when they came down to the river the Neck was sitting on the water, weeping and lamenting. They then said to him, 'Neck, do not grieve so; our father says that your Redeemer liveth also.' The Neck then took his harp and played most sweetly, until long after the sun was gone down.

A Swedish ballad, 'Duke Magnus and the Mermaid', paints a grimmer picture: the sea woman begs for the nobleman's love, crying repeatedly:

Duke Magnus, Duke Magnus, plight thee to me,
I pray you still so freely;
Say me not nay, but yes, yes!

He replies that he would gladly do so 'If thou wert of Christian kind', but as she is 'a vile sea-troll', he can never love her. In that case, says the mermaid, he will lose his wits: the historical Duke Magnus in question, a member of the royal Vasa family, apparently died mad, the ballad's legend being presumably a back-story explaining his insanity.

The dilemma of a man tempted by a sea-maiden but concerned for his own spiritual welfare was explored by Oscar Wilde in an extraordinary and beautiful fable, 'The Fisherman and his Soul' (1891). The fisherman adores a mermaid and begs her to marry him, but she says (a mirror image of Duke Magnus's admirer) that she could only love him if he had *no* soul, since she has none herself. He therefore sends his soul away, though it implores him not to do so. Without his soul, the fisherman has three years of bliss with his beloved: the soul, meanwhile, separated from the fisherman's heart and human emotions, wanders about the world committing acts of evil. When it returns to him, the fisherman becomes wicked too, and only much later, when he sees the mermaid's corpse, is he redeemed. His heart breaks, and to signal heaven's forgiveness, flowers blossom from the grave where he and the mermaid are buried together.

This is unorthodox, to put it mildly, and to a modern reader signals Wilde's conflicted attitude to love and religion. Folktales take a more black-and-white view. In a tale from the Orkneys, told in a collection published in 1954, a young man called Johnnie Croy is said to have married a mermaid, who went off to her own people in the sea seven years later, taking Johnnie and all her children with her: all, that is, except the youngest, who was 'protected' by Johnnie's mother by being branded on the bottom with a red-hot cross, the sacred sign meaning that the sea-woman could not touch him. Whatever one may think of the grandmother, the mermaid was clearly unredeemable.

On the other side of the argument is the case of a mermaid seen swimming near the Hebridean island of Benbecula in about 1820. This creature looked like a miniature woman, being about the size of a four-year-old child but with fully developed breasts. She had long dark hair, soft white skin, and a tail like that of a salmon, but scaleless. The reason she could be described in such detail was that she died, after some boys threw stones at her. She was then buried in a shroud and coffin, which suggests that people considered her more human than animal, though since she was not laid in the churchyard but near the beach where her body was found, perhaps there was some doubt in the matter.

Heinrich Vogeler, illustration to Oscar Wilde's
'The Fisherman and his Soul' (1891)

In John Swan's *Speculum Mundi* (1635) there is recorded the history of a 'Sea-woman' caught in a broken dyke near Edam in the Netherlands, in the early fifteenth century. Brought to land,

> she suffered her self to be clothed, fed with bread, milk, and other meats, and would often strive to steal again into the sea, but being carefully watched she could not: moreover she learned to spin, and perform other petty offices of women; but at the first they cleansed her of the sea-mosse which did stick about her. She was brought from *Edam* and kept at *Harlem*, where she would obey her Mistris, and (as she was taught) kneel down with her before the crucifix, never spake, but lived dumb and continued alive (as some say) fifteen years; then she died.

St Olaf slays the mermaid in the Icelandic *Flateyjarbók* (*c.*1390)

Since she could kneel at the cross, we must suppose that she was capable of salvation.

The origins of fairy beings were sometimes said to be heavenly. According to folk accounts, when the evil angel Lucifer rebelled against God and was cast down to hell, not all his followers went with him: some became fairies on land, and others, turned into mermaids and selkies, found refuge in the sea. If they hadn't been condemned to eternal damnation, did that mean they could ultimately be redeemed? Or were they minor demons, allowed to come into contact with mankind only in order to tempt them?

A 'sea ogress' (*margýgr*) encountered by Olaf, eleventh-century king and later patron saint of Norway, was certainly devilish. Below the waist she looked like a whale, above, like a woman, and she had not only killed many men but destroyed a whole fleet of ships. When she attacked Olaf, the saint speared her (or, say others, cut her head off), his god-given power allowing him to overcome where others before him had failed.

Another mermaid, however, became a saint herself. Liban (meaning 'beauty of women') was a princess whose whole family was drowned when a well overflowed, creating Lough Neagh. The story, from a twelfth-century manuscript, tells how Liban lived on under the lake in a chamber – her *grianan* in Irish, charmingly rendered by one translator as her boudoir – until, fed up with confinement, she prayed

Carved mermaid from Kilcooley Abbey, Tipperary, Ireland (twelfth century)

to be changed into a salmon. Her wish was granted, and with a fish's tail but a woman's head and torso, she spent the next three hundred years swimming about the ocean accompanied by the only other survivor of the flood, her faithful lapdog (transformed into an otter). At the end of this time she sought out a monk to baptise her, was given the name *Muirgein*, 'born of the sea', or *Muirgelt*, 'traverser of the sea', died, and went to heaven, and her grave at Bangor monastery was the site of miracles.

This is one of several Irish legends in which someone from remote history lives on for a miraculously long time and meets monks or missionaries, providing a link between the Christian era and the pagan past. There are also many other tales of lakes created by overflowing springs. Representative of both these traditions, the story of Liban carries a third message too, telling us that there was nothing inherently impossible, to the medieval imagination, in the idea of a holy mermaid.

Another medieval Irish manuscript deals with the descendants of Cain, son of Adam and Eve, and murderer of his brother Abel. According to this source, Cain's daughter Ambia had 'the shape of a woman and the tail of a fish'. Ambia was impregnated by a trout, which 'squirted its spawn into her mouth', and from this unnatural union came the races of leprechauns and giants.

The concept of Cain's monstrous offspring derives ultimately from the Apocrypha, texts not included in the canonical Bible, and was discussed by other medieval clerics as well as the anonymous Irish author, though mermaids are only rarely mentioned. More often, the term 'monsters' was

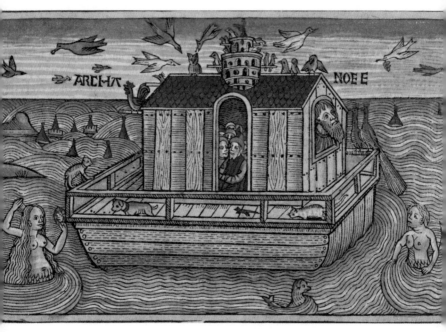

Woodcut showing Noah's ark with mermaids, from the
Nuremberg Bible (fifteenth century)

used of oddly shaped races said to live in remote countries
– remote, that is, from the native lands of early travellers.
Monocoli or Sciapods, with one foot on which they hopped
very fast, and which they used to shield themselves from
the sun; Androgyni who could have sex as men or women;
people who had one eye in their forehead or two in their
shoulders; all these were widely reported as living in India
or Africa, along with pygmies and cannibals who were
considered equally alien. The fifth-century theologian
Augustine debated whether such beings were fully human,

and though he reached no firm conclusion either way, he did not rule out the idea that they were 'descended from Adam', and thus eligible for redemption.

Less open-minded authorities argued that anomalous creatures, neither man nor beast, were evidently cursed. Their monstrosity, a deviation from God's original blessed creation, marked them out as emblems of evil, and even as artistic conceits they were to be avoided. The Latin poet Horace objected to their depiction in verse or image: when 'what is a beautiful woman in the upper part terminates unsightly in an ugly fish below', he wrote in his *Art of Poetry* (*c.*19 BC), unity and harmony are violated.

Those who believed in the physical existence of hybrids and other anomalies, and that they were descended from Cain, inheriting their ancestor's primal sin, were sometimes puzzled by how such creatures had survived the Biblical Deluge, sent expressly to wipe out evil. An elegant solution was that they were aquatic, a tradition that inspired the Irish text discussed above, and one reflected in certain medieval illustrations in which Noah's Ark is seen floating on a sea populated with mermaids.

Eight

FRESHWATER MERMAIDS

Although we tend to think of mermaids as sea-women, 'mer' comes from Old English 'mere', which can mean either the sea or a pool, and mermaids are reported to live in lakes, springs and streams as well as in the ocean. In England, many local water-spirits were named – Jenny Greenteeth in the Lake District, Nelly Long-Arms in Yorkshire, Peg Powler in the River Tees – and feared well into the twentieth century by children whose parents and nurses wanted to keep them away from deep water. Tales of such creatures were intentionally gruesome, to function as warnings: Don't go near the pond or Jenny Greenteeth will pull you in and eat you.

Similar legends seem to be alive in South Africa, where an encounter with a Kaaiman, a half-human half-fish creature that is supposed to be responsible for drownings, was reported in 2008. Daniel Cupido, a resident of Suurbraak in the Western Cape, said that while with his family and friends by the Buffelsjags river, he saw 'a white woman with long black hair thrashing about in the water' (like Mami Wata, the Kaaiman is described as white-skinned):

> Thinking to save her, he waded toward her, but said he stopped in his tracks when he noticed a reddish shine in her eyes.

Theodor Kittelsen, *Nökken* (1904)

She made a sound like crying, so sorrowful, said Daniel's mother Dina, that 'my heart could take it no more'. Dina's husband said their parents had warned them about this creature, but none of them had believed it existed until they saw it for themselves.

Probably all nations have something similar in their repertoire, designed to deter children from taking silly risks. In Russian tales, it was said that if you went near the dark forest pools, a maiden called a rusalka would drag you down to the bottom, or tickle you to death; the Scandinavian Nökke or Neck, while sometimes reported to be a rather gentle and musical spirit, had a more sinister side, as shown in Theodor Kittelsen's painting *Nökken* (the Nökke).

Dutch tradition names several such creatures, as recorded by Mia Gerhardt in *Old Men of the Sea* (1967):

I am acquainted myself with oral tradition from North Holland concerning *Jantje Langarm* ('Johnny Long-arm', mainly a children's bogey), while the most casual enquiry among colleagues immediately produced first-hand information about a *Jan'Aek* or *Jantje den Aker* ('John with the hook') from Zeeland ... In the very recent period here referred to, the general idea was that of a being ... which lurked under water and reached out with a long arm to pull people in and drown them. Dutch children used to be – and, as I was informed, in some regions still are – scared away from canals and water-holes by this effective menace.

The carnivorous appetite of these freshwater creatures is demonstrated in a cautionary tale from Robert Chambers' *Popular Rhymes of Scotland* (1826). The laird of Lorntie in Forfarshire, riding past a loch, hears desperate cries for help and sees a woman apparently about to drown. He is wading in to rescue her, when his servant grabs him, shouting that this is a mermaid. Baulked of her prey, the lady gives a fiendish yell:

'Lorntie, Lorntie,
Were it na your man
I had gart your heart's bluid
Skirl in my pan.'

But for the servant, she's saying, his blood would have sizzled in her cooking pot.

Water sources, however, are not only places of potential danger. Traditionally, they are often sacred, and in many places rags of coloured cloth are still tied to trees near 'healing springs', or coins thrown into 'wishing wells'. Water and women are often linked in ancient Greek and Roman culture, springs and fountains being traditionally guarded or

llustration by Vera Pavlova, made in 1996, to
A.M. Remizov's book of fairytales *Posolon* (1907)

inhabited by nymphs and naiads, and the same affinity holds
good for the medieval Church, with many wells dedicated
to the Virgin and female saints. The water blessed by their
influence was thought to cure many ills, from eye trouble and
skin disease to insanity.

It has been suggested that after the Reformation, when
pagan superstition and Catholic saint-worship alike were
condemned by the Protestant establishment, the guardians
of such holy fountains came to be thought of as elvish,
malevolent beings, helping to explain the savage nature
of the freshwater mermaid. If that were so, you might

expect to find some holy or healing wells, plenty of which remain known, associated in folklore with a resident water-creature. That does not seem to be the case; it is, however, true that some freshwater mermaids are explicitly ascribed a knowledge of medicine and healing.

One of these, the subject of a celebrated Welsh legend, is known as 'The Lady of Van Pool' or 'The Lady of the Van', although the Carmarthenshire lake concerned is properly spelt Fan Fach Lake or Llyn y Fan Fach. From its waters one day emerged a lovely girl, who was courted by a local farmer and agreed to marry him, but who promised that if he struck her three blows without cause, she would leave him for ever.

A warning issued in a fairytale is always fulfilled, and sure enough, he did hit her three times, once for lingering before a christening, once for crying at a wedding, and once for laughing at a funeral. She explained the last two herself – marriage is the beginning of a couple's suffering, a cause for tears, and death ends all troubles, so one should be merry at a funeral – while her reluctance to attend a christening was probably due to its being a sign of acceptance into the Church, and thus a barrier to the supernatural. 'Three causeless blows' feature in other folktales, and (leaving aside questions of domestic violence) generally signal the different perspectives of a fairy pagan wife and a mortal Christian husband, since she laughs at what he sees as misfortune, or cries when he thinks she should be happy.

After the third blow, the mermaid returned to her lake, leaving her husband and three sons on their farm in Myddfai, but later she appeared to her sons and taught them medicine, showing them where herbs should be picked and instructing them in remedies. For centuries, the descendants of the

M.L. Williams, *The Lady of Van Lake* (*c.*1912)

family remained famous as the Physicians of Myddfai.

Two medieval traditions are mingled here: first, a narrative of the twelfth century in which a lady from a Welsh lake takes a human husband, only to leave him after he has hit her (just once, in the earliest version), but years later rescues her son from death and takes him to her watery home; second,

THE SABRINIAN SEA

Bresan

Hatle

Camel

R°
H

The Sorlinges

Cohor

Vale

CORNWAL

Fey

Rosland Promontory

St: Micheales Mount

Menedge
Promontory

THE FRENCH

gon Serk

William Hole, map of Cornwall and Devon drawn to illustrate
Michael Drayton's *Poly-Olbion* (1612). The Bristol Channel appears as
the 'Sabrinian Sea': in Drayton's mythological scheme, Sabrina is the
goddess of the river Severn (see p.99).

accounts of the Myddfai Physicians, real historical figures who were famous in the fourteenth century and still locally renowned at least into the 1960s. Supernatural ancestry was not attributed to them until the mid nineteenth century, when the different strands came together in the story as told above.

A few more medical mermaids appear in nineteenth-century Scottish legend. One nymph emerged from the River Clyde to declare that taking decoctions of nettles and mugwort would protect against consumption: this was considered sound advice, as mugwort, a plant known to botanists as *Artemisia vulgaris*, was traditionally supposed to have curative properties. The Mermaid of Galloway, who frequented both sea and rivers, had similar counsel for a young man whose sweetheart was on the point of death. He gave the girl juice from the mugwort flower, and her life was saved.

In a separate tale, however, the same Galloway mermaid was persecuted by a Christian matron who was so distressed at the nymph's habit of delivering her 'healing oracles' from a stone seat in Dalbeattie Burn, Kirkcudbright, that with Bible in hand she threw down the mermaid's rock. The result was a curse: her baby was found dead in its cradle next morning, and no other child was born to the family. Recorded in an early nineteenth-century collection of local folklore, this tragic fable reflects the Presbyterian zeal of south-west Scotland, where many old beliefs were frowned on by the reformers.

Similar attitudes are expressed, though less violently, in a Japanese legend recorded in the 1920s. An old woman with miraculous healing powers was suspected to be possessed by the spirit of a water-demon, and her neighbours, spying on her at night, said that she changed herself into a white mist and disappeared down a well. Protective charms were then spoken over the well, and the woman never came back, but her house was said to be haunted for years afterwards.

It's occasionally implied that saltwater mermaids too had medical skill. A somewhat ironic story, from John Gregorson Campbell's *Superstitions of the Highlands and Islands of Scotland* (1900), deals with a man from North Harris who caught a mermaid, and was granted three wishes before he released her:

> He became a skilful herb-doctor, who could cure the king's evil [scrofula] and other diseases ordinarily incurable, a prophet, who could foretell, particularly to women, whatever was to befall them, and he obtained a remarkably fine voice. This latter gift he had only in his own estimation; when he sang, others did not think his voice fine or even tolerable.

Mermaids could always sing beautifully, and were often said to predict the future, so we can assume that the third gift of healing was also associated particularly with mermaids.

A few freshwater mermaids were, or became, thought of as personifications of the rivers they inhabited. The Rhine's Lorelei is a case in point, and another, entirely beneficent, is the mermaid of the Severn. Geoffrey of Monmouth's twelfth-century history of Britain tells how Habren, daughter of King Locrine and Estrildis, a German princess, was drowned by Locrine's jealous first wife, and the river where she died became known, after her, as the Habren or Sabrina. In modern English, this became the Severn.

Using the river's Latin name as that of the princess-turned-nymph, poets of the sixteenth and seventeenth centuries adopted 'Sabrina' as a symbol of purity. Spenser's

Peter Hollins, statue of Sabrina (presented 1879) in
the Dingle, Shrewsbury Quarry

Faerie Queene (1590) emphasises her virgin innocence, and
in Drayton's topographical poem *Poly-Olbion* (1612) she is
described as the goddess of the river, ideas developed by
Milton in his masque *Comus* (1634), which gives her a role
as rescuer of a virtuous Lady from the wiles of a sensual
kidnapper. As presiding spirit of the waters, she is invoked
in the lovely lines:

> Sabrina fair
> Listen where thou art sitting
> Under the glassy, cool, translucent wave,
> In twisted braids of lilies knitting
> The loose train of thy amber-dropping hair,
> Listen for dear honour's sake,
> Goddess of the silver lake,
> Listen and save.

Nine
MÉLUSINE

Sabrina's remained a largely literary legend. Although in the eighteenth century there were reports of a mermaid seen swimming in the Bristol Channel, a possible indication that the River Severn was thought to have a resident nymph, she has had little resonance in wider popular tradition.

The medieval tale of another freshwater spirit, by contrast, was highly influential. An early and comparatively plain version appears in Gervase of Tilbury's *Otia Imperialia*, written in the early thirteenth century to provide entertainment and instruction for Otto IV, Holy Roman Emperor (hence the title, translated as 'Recreation for an Emperor').

Gervase writes that Raymond, lord of Rousset in Provence, one day met a beautiful woman by the river Lar. Struck by her charms, he 'began in the usual way to urge her in a gallant speech to give way to his desire'. She held out for marriage, promising that he would enjoy success and happiness as long as he never saw her naked. Raymond agreed, and his fortunes flourished accordingly: 'loved by his friends, held in esteem by all, he embellished his kindness with a discreet generosity and courtesy, and he became the father of very good-looking sons and daughters.' After several years, however, he was suddenly overcome by the wish to look at his wife in her bath. 'Why prolong my tale?' asks Gervase:

> The knight, burning to see his wife naked, snatched away the curtain which screened the bath. The lady immediately turned into a serpent. Plunging her head under the bath-water, she disappeared and was never seen again, nor heard, except sometimes at night, when she came to see her little children; the nurses heard her, but were never able to see her.

As she had warned Raymond, things went from bad to worse for him after that, but his daughter, who married 'a certain kinsman of ours, a scion of the Provençal nobility', was well-loved, and her descendants 'survive to our own day'.

Unnamed in Gervase's version, the lady was later known as Mélusine or Melusina. In the late fourteenth century, legends about her were collected, combined and embellished by Jean d'Arras in a long verse romance, telling essentially the same story, though the ban on Raymond ever seeing his wife naked becomes a prohibition against seeing her at all on a Saturday – the day she turns into a snake. The fateful revelation still takes place while she is bathing:

> Down to her navel, she had the form of a woman, gracefully combing her hair. But from the navel down, her body had the form of a serpent's tail. As big around as a barrel for storing herring, it was, and tremendously long. She lashed the water so forcefully with the tail that it made it splash all the way up to the vaulted ceiling of the chamber. Seeing this, Raymond felt a great sadness.

Unaware that she has been exposed, she does not immediately disappear, but later Raymond reveals that he knows her double

'Mélusine's secret discovered', fifteenth-century illustration to Jean d'Arras' *Le Roman de Mélusine*

nature, and she flies away in the form of a winged serpent.

The important development is concerned with location and relationship: d'Arras tells us that the couple lived in the castle of Lusignan, built by Mélusine herself, and that after leaving Raymond she returned to hover over the battlements, wailing, whenever one of the family was about to die. This

L'IXEMBOVRG EM-
PEREVRS ROYS DE
BOHEME ET HON
GRIE.

LVSIGNANS ROIS
DE IERVSALEM CI
PRE ET ARMENIE.

Mélusine carrying the arms of Luxembourg/Bohemia
and Lusignan/Cyprus, from Estienne de Lusignan, *La Généalogie
des 67 très illustres maisons* (1586)

makes her an ominous hereditary apparition like the Irish
banshee or the White Ladies of German tradition, and
enabled the family of Lusignan to claim her as an ancestor.

So popular, indeed, was her legend that several other
noble families apparently altered their pedigrees to show
a relationship with Mélusine: those who did so must have
felt that they derived distinction, supernatural protection, or
even special powers from the connection (perhaps as in more
recent times, Scottish and Irish families have been proud to
acknowledge the blood-line of the selkies). Even Gervase of
Tilbury couldn't resist linking himself with her, boasting that
'a certain kinsman of ours' had married her daughter.

Although Mélusine is described as half-*serpent* rather than
half-*fish*, she always appears by a river (in Gervase's account)
or by a spring (in later versions), and is revealed in her hybrid

Julius Hübner, *The Beautiful Mélusine* (1844)

form when in her bath: she is clearly a water-spirit, and has always been classed among the mermaids. The family of Lusignan took as their crest the image of a Siren combing her hair and holding a mirror, like a traditional mermaid. Numerous other members of the nobility, all over Europe and Britain, have or had coats of arms featuring tailed women, and certainly in the stylised images of heraldry, it's hard to tell whether the tails are supposed to be piscine or serpentine. Actually, as already noted, the distinction hardly matters: a mermaid is a mermaid, whether her lower half is that of a fish or a reptile.

The story itself migrated, the lady becoming both more dangerous and more definitively a classic mermaid. An early seventeenth-century version sets the scene in Italy, during the reign of King Roger of Sicily (i.e. in the early twelfth century). A man out for an evening swim finds a beautiful woman in the sea, whom he brings to shore and takes home, where after a while she bears him a son. Never, in all the time that she is with him, does she utter a word, and one day a friend suggests that she is not a real woman, but a spectre. Alarmed, he threatens her with his sword to make her speak. She says that by forcing her to do so, he has lost a good wife, and vanishes, only to reappear some years later when her son is playing by the sea. She drags the child into the waves and drowns him.

The affinity with *Undine* and with later tales of mermaid and selkie brides does not mean that all such stories were inspired by that of Mélusine. The thirteenth-century account of King Vilkinus and the mermaid tells, in essence, the same story of a water-nymph who has intercourse with a man, gives birth, and later disappears. If the framework of Mélusine's history is sketched in yet sparer terms, it matches the classical tale of Cupid and Psyche: a supernatural being marries a mortal on condition that the mortal doesn't see the spouse, and leaves when the condition is broken. The plot is obviously ancient, and has taken a wide variety of forms, of which the myth of Mélusine is only one; but her romance was so popular throughout the Middle Ages and beyond that it can be regarded as one of the foundations of modern mermaid legend.

Ten

A FISHY AND FEMININE MIXTURE

Sir Thomas Browne wrote in 1646 that 'Few eyes have escaped the Picture of Mermaids . . . with womans head above, and fishy extremity below.' Browne had no belief in any living creature answering that description, and little interest in mermaid myths, interpreting what he calls a 'fishie and feminine mixture' purely in art-historical terms, as an image derived from classical and archaic sculpture.

Generally, in the seventeenth century and earlier, mermaids function visually as symbol rather than character. The qualities they represent are heterogeneous. At their simplest, they stand for the beauties of watery nature. The Renaissance vogue for all things classical meant that Roman and Greek images of sea-nymphs and tritons were much imitated, often for example incorporated into the design of fountains, while Italian workshops produced a profusion of ornamental items in mermaid form.

Many of these, such as candlesticks and door knockers, have a double rather than single tail, and can appear strikingly rude, with their extremities spread to display what sometimes looks like a foliate vulva, an effect that is surely deliberate. The two-tailed breed has a long history, as well as a prominent

Floor fragment (*c.*1213) from the Basilica of St John
the Evangelist, Ravenna, Italy

modern presence (it figures, of course, on the Starbucks logo,
and is also the model adopted for the Copenhagen statue of
the Little Mermaid, although her finned legs are discreetly
folded beneath her). Archaic images of mermaids were
much influenced by representations of Scylla, the many-
legged monster Odysseus escaped just after he encountered
the Sirens: her tentacles became stylised as two tails, and
Etruscan and Byzantine art in particular continued to show
mermaids or Sirens in that shape.

On pictorial maps, mermaids stood for the exotic and alien.
As a drawing of a dragon or lion indicated territory containing

Diego Gutiérrez, *Map of the Americas* (1562)

unfamiliar dangers, so that of a fishtailed woman meant uncharted oceans and the lure of the yet-to-be-explored. Those who believed in the existence of genuine mermaids could easily suppose that these might be found in foreign waters, and some mariners who saw Sirens, or thought they did – Christopher Columbus and Richard Whitbourne, among others – were not unduly surprised.

Actually, however, rather than discovering mermaids abroad, the pioneers seem to have been exporting them, or more accurately their images, on maps and as ships' figureheads. Mermaids carved as church decoration in Peru, Bolivia and Chile were probably copied by Andean artists from pictures or models the Spanish Jesuits brought with them, and the same sort of cultural transfer probably accounts for West African ideas about Mami Wata and her aquatic kindred as being fair-skinned, although here it seems that Western notions of mermaids mingled with native legends of water-spirits to create a composite Afro-Caucasian Siren.

In heraldry, a mermaid on a coat of arms generally signalled an ancestor famous for his maritime exploits; unless, that is, it belonged to one of those families claiming descent from Mélusine, whose history was so well known that on the Continent a heraldic mermaid was generally known as a *Mélusine*. These too often had a double tail.

Piero di Cosimo's *Allegory* (*c.*1480–90) shows a two-tailed woman wallowing ungracefully below an angel who is tethering, with a very delicate string, a stallion. The picture's composite message seems to be one of Virtue effortlessly mastering brute Nature, in the person of the horse, and trampling on Vice, represented by the mermaid.

That this was, or became, the primary meaning attached to the Siren, pictorially, is clear for instance from the frontispiece to a seventeenth-century code of conduct, Richard Brathwait's *English Gentleman*. It includes a portrayal of Youth, represented (as described in Brathwait's accompanying notes) by a young man

> with a fresh, cheerefull and amiable countenance, seated on a mount, environed with two opposite Rockes: on the right hand stands *Vertue*, with a Palme or Olive branch in her hand . . . On the left hand stands a *Siren*, appearing to the halfe body, with haire dishevelled; who with an attractive aspect reflects on *Youth*.

In the actual illustration, the Siren appears not just 'to the halfe body' but all the way down to the tail, and brandishes

Piero di Cosimo, *Allegory* (*c.*1480–90)

her trademark comb and mirror. Her position opposite Virtue means that she signifies Vice.

The same identification is made in Milton's *Paradise Lost*, when, in Book 2, Satan finds the gates of hell guarded by a terrible Shape that

Richard Westall, 'Death Leaving the Gates of Hell for the
World of Man' (1795), illustration to *Paradise Lost*

seemed woman to the waist, and fair,
But ended foul in many a scaly fold,
Voluminous and vast – a serpent armed
With mortal sting.

She tells Satan that she is his own child, Sin.

There's no contradiction for Milton with his use of Sabrina to personify purity (see Chapter 8): a tailless water-nymph was quite unrelated, in his scheme, to the half-snake figure of cosmic doom. It's the tail that makes the difference, a point that is clear from earlier poetry in which the mermaid or Siren is an emblem of unsanctified desire and heartlessness, her beauty misleading, her song a temptation. In a sonnet to a cruel beloved, Michael Drayton (1563–1631) accuses her:

Three sorts of Serpents doe resemble thee,
That daungerous eye-killing Cockatrice,
Th'inchaunting Syren, which doth so entice,
The weeping Crocodile: these vile pernicious three.
The Basiliske his nature takes from thee,
Who for my life in secrete waite do'st lye,
And to my hart send'st poyson from thine eye,
Thus do I feele the paine, the cause, yet cannot see.

Faire-mayd no more, but Mayr-maid be thy name,
Who with thy sweet aluring harmony
Hast played the thiefe, and stolne my hart from me,
And like a Tyrant mak'st my griefe thy game.
Thou Crocodile, who when thou hast me slaine,
Lament'st my death, with teares of thy disdaine.

The basilisk or cockatrice is a mythical reptile which kills with a glance; a crocodile's tears are still proverbially insincere. To Drayton, these and the Siren or mermaid all count as 'serpents', and similarly, Philip Sidney's *Defence of*

Poesy (*c.*1581–3) mentions 'a siren's sweetness drawing the mind to the serpent's tail of sinful fancies', reinforcing the idea that snaky and fishy hybrids were essentially the same thing, both Sirens.

Lechery was regarded as such a feminine vice that oversexed males too could be called Sirens, in no complimentary sense. J. Sylvester's verse 'On Lovers', from a collection published in 1600, looks at first as if it's talking about homosexuality, but read on and you find that virgin girls are the intended victims of these predatory men:

> Who with a mayden voice, and mincing pace,
> Quaint lookes, curl'd locks, perfumes and painted face,
> Base coward hart, and wanton soft array,
> Their manhood onely by their beard bewray,
> Are cleanly call'd, who likeliest greedy Goates
> Brothell from bed to bed; whose Syren notes
> Inchaunt chast Susans, and like hungry Kite
> Fly at all game, they Lovers are behight.

Rarely, Sirens could be regarded as celestial beings. In a sonnet to his beloved Laura, the fourteenth-century Italian poet Petrarch imagines her a Siren of heaven, whose voice has the power of life and death over him – a concept partly derived from Plato's *Republic* (fourth century BC), which gives a description of the cosmos as formed of concentric rings, one for every planet, each accompanied by a singing Siren whose notes together make up 'the music of the spheres'.

That idea may be one of many that inspire a complex Shakespearean image, in a speech from Act II Scene 2 of *A Midsummer Night's Dream*. 'Thou remember'st,' says Oberon to Puck,

Arthur Rackham, *A Midsummer Night's Dream* (1908)

Anonymous caricature of Mary Queen of Scots (Edinburgh, 1567)

Since once I sat upon a promontory,
And heard a mermaid on a dolphin's back,
Uttering such dulcet and harmonious breath,
That the rude sea grew civil at her song;
And certain stars shot madly from their spheres,
To hear the sea-maid's music.

In context, the 'sea-maid's music' has an equivocal effect. Oberon goes on to say that it was just when the mermaid was singing that one of Cupid's arrows missed its mark, striking not a woman but a flower called love-in-idleness, which thus became the powerful aphrodisiac from which all the rest of the play's confusions and infidelities result.

The passage has been interpreted as a veiled allusion to Mary Queen of Scots, once wife to the Dauphin of France, whose title means literally 'dolphin' (in reference to his coat of arms). The stars that shoot from their spheres are supposed to be noblemen, besotted with Mary, who supported her claim to the throne against Elizabeth I.

Whether or not this was Shakespeare's intent, Mary certainly figured as a Siren in a caricature published in Edinburgh in 1567, by which time she was married to her third husband, James Hepburn, Earl of Bothwell, who was said to have murdered her second, Darnley. The picture shows her as a smirking mermaid, above an armoury of daggers bristling around a hare signifying Bothwell, their identities denoted by the initials MR for Maria Regina, her queenly title, and IH for Iacobus (James) Hepburn. The message is obscure, but still decodable: knives mean assassination, and as for the mermaid, she stands for lust and death in one. Why should this be so? The answer can be found in medieval literature and iconography.

Eleven

A MONSTROUS REGIMENT

Until the Reformation, when all images in sacred buildings became for a while taboo, churches and monasteries were decorated with carvings and paintings. As well as stories from the Old and New Testaments, or miracles of the saints, subjects might include real animals, as symbols of the apostles or illustrations of God's creation, and also fantastic creatures: dragons, griffins, imps and mermaids. Some people disapproved: 'what is meant,' demanded St Bernard of Clairvaux in the twelfth century, 'by painting on the walls of the cloister, where the brethren read, those ridiculous monsters of deformed beauty or beautiful deformity?'

The answer was that such images were supposed to provide instruction to the illiterate (almost everyone, that is, except men of the Church). William Durand, thirteenth-century bishop of Mende, took his authority from the sixth-century Pope Gregory the Great to say that 'what writing supplieth to him which can read, that doth a picture in our churches supply to him which is unlearned and can only look.'

The message that the mermaid or Siren was intended to carry was a warning against sin. This was spelt out in

Linocut by John Hinchcliffe of the fifteenth-century
roof boss in Sherborne Abbey, Dorset

bestiaries, catalogues of real and fabulous fauna that were
framed primarily as moral treatises, using the beasts or beings
they described to illustrate spiritual questions. A thirteenth-
century example gives a typical characterisation of the Siren:

> So sweetly does she sing and well
> That they who go sailing on the sea
> As soon as they hear that song,
> Cannot forbear
> From letting their ship approach.
> So soothing seems the song to them.
> That in their ship they fall asleep,
> And when they are so fast asleep,
> Then they are deceived and trapped;
> For the syrens kill them
> Without their uttering shriek or cry.

The author goes on to explain that vices such as gluttony, lust and avarice are snares of the Devil, who lulls our souls asleep:

Then he attacks us, then he falls upon us,
Then he kills us, then he does us to death,
Just as the syrens do
To the mariners who sail the seas.

Figurative use of the Siren or mermaid, as with other mythic hybrids such as the centaur (half-man half-horse), need connote no belief in a corresponding physical reality. It's the very impossibility of such a creature, combining the archetypal qualities of two or more beasts of land and sea or air, that makes for a potent and adaptable emblem capable of conveying a variety of different meanings. Composite Sirens were useful as teaching aids because their double natures supplied a metaphor for man's duality as a god-given spirit united to an animal body, or for the deceptively seductive lures of Satan.

Although this was clear to literate clerics, to an unlettered congregation the visible presence of Sirens around the pews might be taken straightforwardly to imply that mermaids were church-goers. St Senara's in Zennor, Cornwall, has a detailed story about a woman who used to attend services there, and inveigled away a handsome parishioner to join her in the sea. On a bench-end there is a fifteenth-century carving of a mermaid: this probably gave rise to the legend, but folklore has reversed cause and effect, so that the carving is pointed out as commemorating the mermaid's visit.

More generally, the sight of Sirens represented alongside eagles, oxen and other flesh-and-blood animals could have suggested that all were equally drawn from nature, giving rise

Above: Siren and Centaur from Hugh of Fouilloy's *Aviarium* (1250–1300)

Below: St Senara's church in Zennor, Cornwall: photograph showing bench-end with fifteenth-century carving of a mermaid

to or supporting belief in mermaids.

To the theologically educated, however, the Siren was symbol rather than reality. The danger posed by Homer's Sirens – that they enticed sailors to their doom – was interpreted by many scholars as signifying sexual allurement, and it was indeed argued that the original Sirens had been neither more nor less than prostitutes. In the *Etymologies*, an influential seventh-century work, Isidore of Seville writes that the Sirens were romanticised as musical beings who would draw mariners to disaster with their song:

> In truth, however, they were harlots, who, because they would seduce passers-by into destitution, were imagined as bringing shipwreck upon them.

Whether literally, as a whore, or figuratively, as personification of lechery, the Siren became identified primarily as carnal temptress, her slithery tail signalling her lubricious promiscuity. The fourteenth-century poet Boccaccio wrote in his *Genealogia*, a collection of mythological lore, that Sirens 'are fish from the navel down, for women are beautiful and honest to the girdle, but all their lust resides in the navel', an accusation later echoed by Shakespeare in *King Lear*:

> But to the girdle do the gods inherit,
> Beneath is all the fiend's; there's hell, there's darkness. . .

Actually the lines just before these, part of Lear's diatribe against women (Act IV Scene 6), assert that 'Down from the waist they are centaurs' – rather than Sirens or mermaids. As may by now have become clear, it doesn't much matter whether the lower half of a woman is fish, bird, snake, or

Twelfth-century sheela-na-gig from
Kilpeck Church, Herefordshire

even horse: the important point is that it is *animal*, with all
that implies about brute appetite and instinct.

Images of the Siren or mermaid, then, were intended to
warn against wantonness. According to recent theory, they
performed another function too, protecting the virtuous
against demons, who, it is argued, were thought liable to be
frightened by the same things that frightened men. Among
such terrors was a display of rampant female sexuality, and this
helps to explain the bizarre phenomenon of sheela-na-gigs,
carvings on churches and castles found most commonly in
Ireland, but also in Britain and France, showing women with
their legs spread to flaunt their genitals. It is also suggestive
when considering some portrayals of two-tailed mermaids

holding their extremities apart: a 'tail' is ambiguous verbally, and can be visually so too. Even the less blatant single-tailed Siren, however, was salacious by her very nature, and thus scared man and devil alike.

That's not to say that the only or even the main reason for showing mermaids was to avert evil. While the apotropaic (protective) power of the mermaid may partly account for her widespread use as church ornament and heraldic emblem, and later as inn sign, ship's figurehead and tattoo, a simpler reason presents itself. Like Victorian painters, earlier artists and craftsmen were partial to topless women; so were viewers, particularly among all-male communities such as monks and sailors, and as for men in pubs . . . enough said.

MARINA INN
St. Leonards-on-Sea

Twelve

SEXING THE SIREN

In modern English, the words 'mermaid' and 'Siren' can be used more or less interchangeably to mean a water-dwelling woman with a fish's tail. Historically, however, these are three distinct matters.

Lines from the *Romaunt of the Rose* establish that by the fourteenth century, the mermaid was thought of as synonymous with the Siren:

> Though we mermaydens clepe hem here
> In English, as in our usaunce,
> Men clepn hem sereyns in Fraunce.
>
> [Though we call them mermaids here
> In English, as is our usage,
> Men call them sirens in France.]

Whether the poet thought that either 'mermayden' or 'sereyn' had a fishtail, we don't know. In Old English, a *merewyf* or *mereminen* was a water-spirit of the tailless variety, and in general, the supernatural aquatic beings of Northern European tradition are human-shaped. Folklore from the medieval period onwards, however, attached tails to many such creatures. Mélusine, for example, has a serpentine lower body, and the Irish Liban is half salmon.

Creatures with fishes' tails below a human torso appear in classical Greek art. Known as tritons and tritonesses, they attend Poseidon and other sea-deities. Their predecessors are Middle Eastern: Mesopotamian cylinder seals from the second millennium BC show male and female fishtailed figures, while an Assyrian relief sculpture of the eighth century BC shows a merman whose horned crown signifies that he is divine. In Babylon, according to a report of the third century BC, a god called Oannes once rose from the sea to impart wisdom: he is described as having the body of a fish, and 'under a fish's head another head, and also feet below, similar to those of a man, subjoined to the fish's tail', suggesting a priest wearing a ceremonial disguise.

A mermaid-goddess, Atargatis or Derceto, had her temple in ancient Syria. Lucian of Samosata writes in the second century AD:

I saw in Phoenicia a drawing, in which she is represented in a curious form; for in the upper half she is woman, but from the waist to the lower extremities runs in the tail of a fish.

From around the third century BC onwards, there are occasional pictorial examples of fishtailed women identified as the Sirens of Homeric myth. This does not, however, become at all usual until much later, and the first mention in literature of a fishtailed Siren comes in the seventh-century *Liber monstrorum* ('Book of monsters'):

Sirens are sea-girls, who deceive sailors with the outstanding beauty of their appearance and the sweetness of their song, and are most like human beings from the head to the navel, with the body of a maiden, but have scaly fishes' tails, with which they always lurk in the sea.

Above: Detail of eighth century BC carving from the palace of Sargon II at Khorsabad, Iraq

Below: Fish-Siren from a thirteenth-century Bestiary

Above: Vase painting of *c.*330 BC, showing Odysseus with bird Sirens

Left: Relief panel from the Tomb of Kybernis, *c.*470-460 BC, from Xanthos (modern Günük, south-western Turkey): a winged Siren carries a small figure, perhaps a soul of the dead (see p.131)

From this point onwards, in both words and images, the fishy Siren begins to supplant her rival, a Siren who is not woman/fish, but woman/*bird*. That is how she figures in the seventh-century *Etymologies* already cited, where Isidore of Seville records that 'People imagine three Sirens who were part maidens, part birds, having wings and talons.' In the *Physiologus*, from the second century AD, it is stated that the Sirens are 'death-dealing creatures dwelling in the sea':

> Like the Muses, they sing with their voices, and the sailors, when they hear their melody, cast themselves into the sea and perish. They have the form of a woman down to the waist, and the lower half has the appearance of a bird.

These descriptions match the prevalent visual image. Grecian art from the sixth century BC shows the Sirens as having human torsos and arms above birds' bodies, while creatures more completely bird, with just a human head, appear from around a century earlier.

To sum up a fairly complicated sequence, then:

Fishtailed people appear in the art of very early antiquity: they have no generic name, either Siren or mermaid/merman;

Sirens are shown as part human, part bird from the seventh century BC onwards, and this continues to be the prevalent image for the next fifteen hundred years or so;

The Siren as part *fish* first appears in the third century BC. She remains rare until the seventh or eighth century AD, but then becomes progressively more common until she has almost entirely ousted the bird Siren;

From at latest the fourteenth century, 'Siren' means the same as *'mermaid'*, 'mermayden' etc: a water-woman who may or may not have a fishtail, but hardly ever has a bird's wings or claws.

When considering the metamorphosis of the Siren, an obvious question is what Homer, in the eighth century BC, has to say about her appearance.

Nothing at all, is the answer. Going back to the original *Odyssey*, or a literal translation, we read first the event foretold by the goddess Circe, and then the event itself, in which Odysseus's ship approaches the Sirens' territory, a meadow strewn with human remains. Warned by Circe that it is fatal to hear the Sirens' song, the crew plug their ears with wax, and Odysseus is tied to the mast. When they row within earshot, the Sirens address Odysseus by name, promising to share with him their knowledge of all that has happened at Troy and everywhere in the world. Odysseus then longs to swim to them, but following his earlier instructions, the crew only bind him tighter, and they sail safely past.

That's it. There's no mention of what the Sirens look like, whether half-bird, half-fish, or anything else. We only know they're female because Greek, a gendered language, can't help telling us so.

Later writers gave the Sirens names and parents, located their island off the west coast of Italy, and added the idea that if they failed to attract any passing voyager, they were fated to die. From the *Odyssey*, however, our prime source, we glean no more than a tradition of the Sirens as female supernaturals, whose defining characteristic is the vocal spell they cast.

For their physical form, we turn to the visual record, which begins by showing the Sirens consistently as hybrid human/

birds. In the earliest examples they do not accompany Odysseus; rather, they tend to appear on tombs and graves, a context that has led scholars to propose an influence from ancient Egyptian images of the 'soul-bird', a face on a feathered body representing the spirit of the departed or its guide to the underworld.

Their relationship to death may be relevant to Homer's portrayal. Certainly his Sirens kill: bones and decaying skin lie around them. How their victims die is left to the imagination, whether their blood is sucked or their flesh eaten, or whether they simply starve while entranced by the magic song.

As to that song, the *Odyssey* is our sole source. Although a fragment attributed to Hesiod, a poet from around the same time as Homer in the eighth century BC, records that the winds themselves responded to the Sirens' voices, only Homer gives us any account of their words. The spell they cast makes men forget their homes and families, Circe warns, and when the Sirens speak in person, they promise Odysseus enlightenment. It is, however, an odd and unsatisfactory form of knowledge they proffer: although they say they know everything that takes place in the world, the only specific they mention is what's happened in the battle at Troy, which Odysseus, who has been at that battle, knows as well as anyone. Perhaps the most enticing thing they warble is the warrior's own name, linked to renown and honour: 'Come hither, much praised Odysseus, glory of the Greeks,' they sing. On one level, what they offer is a reflection of fame, a hymn to a hero's greatness that would sound sweet in that hero's ears: holding up a flattering mirror, you could say. If the sailors didn't have their ears covered, they might have heard their own names crooned just as blandishingly.

The legend of the Sirens' song developed in two ways. Quite soon after Homer's own time, it started to be said that the Sirens played instruments, and that is how they are shown in many images. The musical Siren became proverbial, and singing (generally unaccompanied) is an almost universal feature of later mermaids.

The Sirens' *words*, on the other hand, were originally considered more important than their melody, and became a metaphor for persuasive or delightful speech. Homer himself was called a Siren by later Greek writers, in the sense that he was a marvellous poet. Cicero, writing in the first century BC, said it was the Sirens' offer of knowledge that tempted passing voyagers: from ideas like these, at least in part, come later accounts of prophetic mermaids. It also led to Christian commentators allegorising the Sirens' lures as those of heresy: misleading pronouncements.

The most common interpretation of the Siren, however, among early theologians and ever after, has been as femme fatale, using her sex to seduce. Nothing contributes to that in Homer, nor in most visual representations of the half-bird creature (a few images, indeed, show avian Sirens as bearded males). How then does it come about, the prevalent, almost universal association with feminine wiles? Any word we can use for what the Sirens did – they charmed, allured, enticed, tempted, bewitched – has the same inevitable connotation, and 'Siren' has become a synonym not only for 'mermaid' but for 'dangerously fascinating woman'.

Is it simply that to commentators (men), it was obvious that a woman had nothing nearly so attractive to offer as herself? Knowledge, prophetic or otherwise, comes a poor second, and music can be lovely, but not so lovely as a pair of breasts.

Male bearded Siren, Church of St Peter and St Paul,
Remagen, Germany (twelfth century)

That might be explanation enough, but there's also the
context in which the Sirens first come before us. Book 12
of the *Odyssey*, in which their episode occurs, opens with
a conversation between Odysseus and Circe, a beautiful
goddess with power to enchant men, who has delayed the
hero's voyage for a year while they enjoy an affair. We first learn
about the Sirens from what she says, she accurately predicts
their behaviour, and Odysseus's encounter with them follows
immediately after he has left her, giving the Sirens a close
relationship, in narrative terms, with the goddess. Perhaps the
Sirens, themselves a blank screen on which any picture can be
projected, take colour from beguiling Circe (who also sings a
spellbinding song). That people could and did misremember
what parts of the narrative applied to which character is

Terracotta relief of Scylla, *c.*450BC, from the Cyclades, Greece

demonstrated, for instance, by a passage in Dante's *Purgatorio* where a Siren confesses that she 'turned Ulysses [Odysseus] from his road', which the Sirens didn't, but Circe did.

Apart from Circe, the supernatural female most closely linked to the Sirens, the next peril Odysseus encounters after his escape from them, is Scylla, described by Homer as a ravenous monster who has a yelping canine voice and six heads to bark with. Her twelve feet and all her lower parts are hidden by the sea. In both visual art and literature, Scylla changed over time, mutating into an attractive (one-headed) woman from the waist upwards, her feet or tentacles turned into multiple fishtails, while her doglike barking got transferred to actual dogs, attached to her nether regions. This is how she figures in Virgil's *Aeneid*, in the first century BC:

> In front her face is human, and her breast fair as a maiden's to
> the waist down; behind she is a sea-dragon of monstrous frame,
> with dolphins' tails joined on her wolf-girt belly.

The sexual threat of this imagery was toned down in Etruscan and Byzantine sculpture and painting, which represented Scylla more simply as a double-tailed mermaid. Somehow, this fishy figure became identified as a Siren – probably at least in part because the curvaceous aquatic form suggested her powers of fascination more compellingly than a squat bird's body. What a Siren looks like is intimately connected with what she does: if she tempts to Sin and Vice, then an excellent metaphor is a being who looks from the waist upwards like an inviting woman, but conceals below the water a scaly fish's tail.

Almost anyone, asked about the mermaid's history, will mention Homer's Sirens, and they'd be right, even though the Sirens were *not* mermaids, and originally shared very few of the characteristics we now associate with them. Via complex paths of association and representation, by affinity with Scylla and Circe, through men's assumptions about women and artists' liking for the female semi-nude, the Siren becomes irresistible woman becomes fishtailed temptress becomes mermaid.

Reverting to the original question of how modern mermaids have come to be as they are, the family tree does go back to the *Odyssey*, as we might expect. More surprising, perhaps, is how many relatives the mermaid has that aren't fish. Birds come into the picture from way back with the original Siren, and again as Teutonic swan women, part-human brides taken by fully human husbands. Snakes feature in medieval tales and Renaissance imagery, Biblical associations with both wisdom and temptation making the serpent princess a slippery, powerful partner for a man. Seals and Sirenians, aquatic mammals that can look, remotely, like swimming women, have a mythic repertoire of their own that parallels and has contributed to the mermaid legend.

Still, the half-fish mermaid is the image everyone recognises. Creatures that breathe underwater are alien in a fundamental way, less of our world than bird or beast, because they die in our element, and we in theirs. That the mermaid bridges this divide signals her potency, her otherness, her ambiguity.

The urge to personify and gender nature seems hard-wired into the human psyche. Water nurtures, upholds and transports, but also imperils: humans can't survive in it, nor live without it. Scary beings that lurk in sea or lake or river represent primal fear of the unknown, and given that the mythmakers of history have been men, it comes as no great shock that in many cultures, water and its resident spirits are feminine. Sea tides, influenced by the moon as women's menstruation goes in a roughly lunar cycle, make a compelling analogy, and then there are all the other terms, changeable and spellbinding, deathdealing and lifegiving, applied through the ages to both women and water.

Water's lovely to look at and a delight to swim in, and its women inhabitants might be malign but also alluring, not just waiting to pull men under by force, but able to make them desire their drowning. Here is the birth of the fatally attractive Siren who offers pleasure, but really means only to satisfy her own appetite. From the murderous glutton of the Bestiaries, via Tudor poetry and Victorian art, the line of descent runs right through to the twenty-first-century mermaids who menace Captain Jack Sparrow and his crew in *Pirates of the Caribbean*.

The tree branches at some point; how far back, it's hard to say. Homer makes his most memorable ocean-perils women, whether as Scylla and Charybdis they are hideous monsters, as the Sirens, little but a female voice, or, like Calypso and Circe, beautiful witches. In the case of these last, a sufficiently cunning hero can master the enchantress to get what he wants, and the *Odyssey* may well have had an effect on later legend in this as in many other respects. Certainly in the Middle Ages it became a commonplace that men could possess water-spirits as mistresses or wives, and father children on them. Then the question follows: why should the nymph allow herself to be exploited? Mystical Christian interpretation, that only so could she gain a soul, had resonance down the centuries, and though a Disney toy might not seem at first glance to have much to do with Paracelsus, the ancestry is quite clearly trackable.

That leaves my Spanish Siren, and her rebel sisterhood. In reaction rather than development, the feminist mermaid has quite recently evolved to protest against what the breed has stood for up till now. The Madrid graffiti was painted over soon after I saw her, but her message lives on: I've got breasts, get over it; do your own thing, is her manifesto. I'll say it for her one more time:

DOWN WITH PATRIARCHY!
DON'T GIVE UP ON YOUR LIFE, TAKE CENTRE STAGE!

References

Where page numbers are unstated, references are *passim*. Websites have not been included.

Chapter 1

Andersen (1935); Austern & Naroditskaya (2006) 1–15; Bartholomaeus Anglicus (1976) 380; Cole (2014); Gunderson (1980) 155–6; Hutchins (1968) 7; Udovitch (2000) 47

Chapter 2

Allen (1903) xxxvi-xxxvii; Baring-Gould (1901) 501; Cooper (2009); Dijkstra (1986) 258–71; Fauser (2006); Fouqué (1867); Gervase of Tilbury (2002) 729–31; Haymes (1988) 22–3, 221–2; Heine (1982) 76–7, 849; Ivanits (1989) 62–5; 75–82; Magee (1990) 61–7; *Nibelungenlied* (2004) 192–6, 379; Paracelsus (1964) 67–78; Pushkin (2007); Silver (1999); Thackeray (1985) 738

Chapter 3

A.J.C. (n.d.); Almqvist (1990); Bastian (1998) 21–31; Campbell (1900) 201–2; Craigie (1896) 221–4, 436–7; Croker (1838) 196–205; Drewal (1988) 101–139; Drewal, Gore & Kisliuk (2006); Heaney (1993); Ibsen (1907); Newell (2003); *Nibelungen Noth* (1843) 211; *Nibelungenlied* (2004) 192–6; Pontoppidan (1755) 186–90; Pope (1907) 180; Roud & Bishop (2012) 32–3, 385–7; [Swan] (1665) 333–4; Thorpe (1852) Vol. 2, 27–8, 173; Wagner (1900?); Wells (2002); Ystad (1998)

Chapter 4

Bruford & MacDonald (1994) 477; Campbell (1900) 283–4; Craigie (1896) 231–3, 436–7; Davies (1978) 27; Grimm (1999) Vol. 1, 426–31; Henderson (1910) 98, 260–66; Hibbert (1822) 551, 566–71; Kennedy-Fraser (1929) 189–90; MacCodrum (1938) xxxiv–xliv; MacRitchie (1890) 1–17; Ó hÓgáin (2006) 342–5; O'Sullivan (1974) 116–19; Scoresby (1849?) 165–6; Thomson (2001); Thorpe (1852) Vol. 2, 173

Chapter 5

Dietz (1992) 18–20, 83; Gosse (1861) 125–45; Hamilton (1839) 285–91; Lee (1884) 213–20; Morgan (1989) 65–6; Morgan (1795) 302–6; Morison (1963) 148; Powell (2002); Renard (1754) Plate LVII; Scoresby (1849?) 163; *The Times*, 8.9.1809, 3; Vinycomb (1906) 232–3; Weiss & Buchanan (2009) 6, 29, 120, 239; Whitbourne (1622) conclusion (unnumbered)

Chapter 6

Alderson (1992) 32–4; Altick (1978) 302–3; Baring-Gould (1876) 17–21; Buckland (1860) 226–7, 313–14; Chambers (1888) Vol. 2, 266; Dance (1976) 17–18, 43–53; Dunsany (1978); *Gentleman's Magazine* Vol. 29 (1759) 590, Vol. 45 (1775) 216, Vol. 92, (1822) 82–3, 366, 461–2, 516, 548–60, Vol. 93 (1823) 34–9; Gosse (1861) 125–45; Vickers & Dionne (2007)

Chapter 7

Augustine (1965) 49; Carmichael (1928) Vol. 2, 326; Friedman (1981) 98–9; Gervase of Tilbury (2002) 729–31; Horace (1882) 203; Johnsen (1922) 14–16 (translated here by Terry Gunnell); Joyce (1894) 97–105; Keightley (1850) 147–50; Montgomerie (1956) 101; O'Donovan (1851) Vol. 1 201–3; Pliny (2012) Vol. 1, 325–32; Rodway (2010); Stewart (1823) 57; Thorpe (1852) Vol. 2, 27–8; Turville-Petre (1953) 176–7; Wilde (1891)

Chapter 8

Campbell (1900) 201–2; Chambers (1870) 330–32; Cromek (1810) 229–32; Dijkstra (1986) 258–71; Geoffrey of Monmouth (2007) 32–5; Gerhardt (1967) 48–51; Gwyndaf (1992–3) 60–1; Keightley (1850) 409–11; Macculloch (1932) 52–3; Mackenzie (1923) 85–6; Map (1924) 91–4; Miller (1988) 190–92; Milton (1968) esp. 76; Rhys (1980) Vol. 1, 2–74; Thorpe (1852) Vol. 2, 77–8; Woodhouse & Bush (1972) 956-9

Chapter 9

d'Arras (2007) Vol. 2, esp 563–4; Baring-Gould (1901) 471–523; Gervase of Tilbury (2002) 88–91; Keightley (1850) 450; Macculloch (1932) 49–51

Chapter 10

Brathwait (1630) 1; Browne (1981) Vol. 1, 415–18; Drayton (1861) 164; Luchs (2010); Milton (1877) 75–7; Moule (1842) 213–19; Okada (2006); Petrarch (1965) 149; Plato (1852) 413; Rachewiltz (1987); Sidney (2002) 234; Sylvester (1970); Vinycomb (1906) 223–275

Chapter 11

Andersen (1977); Buhler (2006); Durand (2007) 32; Gregory (2004) Vol. 3, 745; Luchs (2010); Luddy (1927) 109; Mellinkoff (2004) Vol. 1, esp. 39–49, 63–7, 137–42; Rachewiltz (1987); de Thaun (1841) 98; Westwood & Simpson (2005) 119-22

Chapter 12

Adler & Tuffin (2002) 38–9; Cicero (1914) 448–51; Dante (1880) 226–9; Gosse (1861) 125–45; Gresseth (1970); Hesiod (2007) 83; Holford-Strevens (2006); Isidore of Seville (2006) 30; Luchs (2010); Lucian of Samosata (1820) 441; *Physiologus* (1924) 207; Rachewiltz (1987); *Romaunt of the Rose* (1911) 9; Vermeule (1979) esp. 75–6, 201, 205; Virgil (2004) 73

Bibliography

A.J.C., 'Married to a Mermaid' (song sheet) (London, *c.*1860)

Adler, William & Tuffin, Paul, eds., *The Chronography of George Synkellos: A Byzantine Chronicle of Universal History from the Creation* (Oxford & New York, 2002)

Alderson, William T. (ed.), *Mermaids, Mummies, and Mastodons: The Emergence of the American Museum* (Washington, 1992)

Allen, J. Romilly, *The Early Christian Monuments of Scotland* (Edinburgh, 1903)

Almqvist, Bo, 'Of Mermaids and Marriages', *Béaloideas* Vol. 58 (Dublin, 1990) 1–74

Altick, Richard D., *The Shows of London* (Cambridge, Mass. & London, 1978)

Andersen, Hans Christian, 'The Little Mermaid', in *Fairy Tales and Legends* (London, 1935) 72–95

Andersen, Jørgen, *The Witch on the Wall: Medieval Erotic Sculpture in the British Isles* (Copenhagen, 1977)

d'Arras, Jean, ed. Matthew W. Morris, *A Bilingual Edition of Jean d'Arras's Mélusine or L'Histoire de Lusignan* (Lewiston, Queenston, Lampeter, 2007)

Augustine, trans. Sanford, Eva Matthews, & Green, William McAllen, Vol. 5 of *Saint Augustine: The City of God against the Pagans*, 7 vols (London & Cambridge, Mass., 1957–72) (Vol. 5 1965)

Austern, Linda Phyllis, & Naroditskaya, Inna, eds, *Music of the Sirens* (Bloomington, 2006)

Baring-Gould, Sabine, *Curious Myths of the Middle Ages* (London etc, 1901) [1866]

—, *The Vicar of Morwenstow: A Life of Robert Stephen Hawker*, 3rd edn (London, 1876)

Bartholomaeus Anglicus, ed. Jürgen Schäfer, *Batman uppon Bartholome His Booke De Proprietatibus Rerum* 1582 (Hildesheim & New York, 1976)

Bastian, Misty L., 'Mami Wata, Mr. White, and the Sirens off Bar Beach: Spirits and Dangerous Consumption in the Nigerian Popular Press', *Afrika und das Andere* (Hamburg, 1998)

Benwell, Gwen, & Waugh, Arthur, *Sea Enchantress: The Tale of the Mermaid and her Kin* (London, 1961)

Brathwait, Richard, *The English Gentleman* (London, 1630)

Browne, Thomas, *Pseudodoxia Epidemica*, ed. Robin Robbins, 2 vols (Oxford, 1981)

Bruford, Alan, and MacDonald, Donald A., *Scottish Traditional Tales* (Edinburgh, 1994)

Buckland, Francis T., *Curiosities of Natural History*, Second Series (London, 1860)

Buhler, Stephen M., 'The Sirens, the Epicurean Boat, and the Poetry of Praise' in Austern & Naroditskaya (2006) 176–93

Campbell, John Gregorson, *Superstitions of the Highlands and Islands of Scotland* (Glasgow, 1900)

Carmichael, Alexander, *Carmina Gadelica*, 5 vols (Edinburgh & London, 1928)

Chambers, Robert, *The Book of Days*, 2 vols (London & Edinburgh, 1888) [1869]

—, *Popular Rhymes of Scotland*, new edn (London & Edinburgh, 1870)

Cicero, *De Finibus Bonorum et Malorum*, trans. Rackham, H. (London & New York, 1914)

Cole, Teju, 'Under the skin', *Guardian* 25.09.2014, 16–17

Cooper, Suzanne Fagence, 'The Liquefaction of Desire: Music, Water and Femininity in Victorian Aestheticism', *Women: A Cultural Review* Vol. 20 No. 2, Summer 2009 (Taylor & Francis, Abingdon, 2009) 186–201

Craigie, William A., *Scandinavian Folk-Lore* (London, 1896)

Croker, Thomas Crofton, *Fairy Legends and Traditions of the South of Ireland*, 2nd edn (London, 1838)

Cromek, R.H., *Remains of Nithsdale and Galloway Song* (London, 1810)

Dance, Peter, *Animal Fakes and Frauds* (Maidenhead, 1976)

Dante Alighieri, *The Purgatory*, trans. Arthur John Butler (London, 1880)

Davies, Brian, *Seal Song* (London, 1978)

Dietz, Tim, *The Call of the Siren: Manatees and Dugongs* (Golden, Colorado, 1992)

Dijkstra, Bram, *Idols of Perversity: Fantasies of Feminine Evil in Fin-de-Siècle Culture* (New York & Oxford, 1986)

Drayton Michael, ed. J. Payne Collier, *Poems by Michael Drayton* (London, 1861)

Drewal, Henry John, 'Interpretation, Invention and Re-presentation in the Worship of Mami Wata', *Journal of Folklore Research* Vol. 25, Nos. 1/2 (Indiana, Jan-Aug 1988) 101–139

Drewal, Henry John, Gore, Charles, & Kisliuk, Michelle, 'Siren Serenades: Music for Mami Wata and Other Water Spirits in Africa' in Austern & Naroditskaya (2006) 294–316

Dunsany, Lord, 'Mrs Jorkens' in *The Travel Tales of Mr. Joseph Jorkens* (London, 1978) [1931] 242–71

Durand, William of Mende, *The Rationale Divinorum Officiorum of William Durand of Mende: A New Translation of the Prologue and Book One*, trans. Thibodeau, Timothy M. (New York, 2007)

Fauser, Annegret, 'Rheinsirenen: Loreley and Other Rhine Maidens' in Austern & Naroditskaya (2006) 250–72

Fouqué, Friedrich de la Motte, 'Undine' in *Undine and Other Tales*, trans. F.E. Bunnett (Leipzig, 1867) 1–106

Friedman, John Block, *The Monstrous Races in Medieval Art and Thought* (Cambridge, Mass, & London, 1981)

Gentleman's Magazine (London, 1731–1922)

Geoffrey of Monmouth, ed. Reeve, Michael D., trans. Wright, Neil, *The History of the Kings of Britain* (An Edition and Translation of *De gestis Britonum*) (Woodbridge, 2007)

Gerhardt, Mia I., *Old Men of the Sea* (Amsterdam, 1967)

Gervase of Tilbury, *Otia Imperialia*: Recreation for an Emperor, ed. & trans. S.E. Banks & J.W. Binns (Oxford, 2002)

Gosse, Philip, *Romance of Natural History*, Second Series (London, 1861)

Gregory the Great, *The Letters of Gregory the Great*, trans. Martyn, John R.C., 3 vols (Toronto, 2004)

Gresseth, Gerald K., 'The Homeric Sirens', *Transactions and Proceedings of the American Philological Association*, Vol. 101 (Princeton, 1970) 203–18

Grimm, Jacob, trans. James Steven Stallybrass, *Teutonic Mythology*, 4 vols (London, 1999) [1835]

Gunderson, Lloyd L., *Alexander's Letter to Aristotle about India* (Meisenheim, 1980)

Gwyndaf, Robin, 'A Welsh Lake Legend and the Famous Physicians of Myddfai', *Béaloideas* (Dublin, 1992–3) 60–1

Hamilton, Robert, *The Natural History of the Amphibious Carnivora* (Edinburgh, London & Dublin, 1839)

Haymes, Edward R., trans., *The Saga of Thidrek of Bern* (New York & London, 1988)

Heaney, Seamus, 'Maighdean Mara' in *Wintering Out* (London, 1993) [1972] 56–7

Heine, Heinrich, trans. Draper, Hal, *The Complete Poems* (Boston, 1982)

Henderson, George, *The Norse Influence on Celtic Scotland* (Glasgow, 1910)

Hesiod, ed. and trans. Glenn W. Most, *The Shield; The Catalogue of Women; Other Fragments* (Cambridge, Mass., & London, 2007)

Hibbert, Samuel, *A Description of the Shetland Islands* (Edinburgh, 1822)

Holford-Strevens, Leofranc, 'Sirens in Antiquity and the Middle Ages' in Austern & Naroditskaya (2006) 16–51

Horace, 'Epistle to the Pisos; or, The Art of Poetry', in *Works*, trans. Roscoe Mongan (London, 1882) 203–16

Hutchins, Jane, *Discovering Mermaids and Sea Monsters* (Tring, 1968)

Ibsen, Henrik, trans. Frances E. Archer, *The Lady from the Sea*, in *Collected Works* (London, 1907) Vol. 9, 165–349

Isidore of Seville, ed. and trans. Barney, Stephen A., et al, *The* Etymologies *of Isidore of Seville* (Cambridge, 2006)

Ivanits, Linda J., *Russian Folk Belief* (New York & London, 1989)

Johnsen, Oscar Albert, *Olafs Saga hins Helga* (Kristiania, 1922)

Joyce, P.W., *Old Celtic Romances* (London, 1894)

Keightley, Thomas, *The Fairy Mythology* (London, 1850)

Kennedy-Fraser, Marjory, *A Life of Song* (London, 1929)

Lee, Henry, 'Sea Fables Explained', *The Fisheries Exhibition Literature* Vol. III (London, 1884) 178–317

Luchs, Alison, *The Mermaids of Venice: Fantastic Sea Creatures in Venetian Renaissance Art* (London & Turnhout, 2010)

Lucian of Samosata, trans. W. Tooke, 'De Dea Syria', in *Works*, 2 vols (London, 1820) Vol. 2, 433–69

Luddy, Ailbe J., *Life and Teaching of St Bernard* (Dublin, 1927)

MacCodrum, John, ed. Matheson, William, *The Songs of John MacCodrum* (Edinburgh, 1938)

Macculloch, J.A., *Medieval Faith and Fable* (London etc, 1932)

Mackenzie, Donald, *Myths of China and Japan* (London, 1923)

MacRitchie, David, *The Testimony of Tradition* (London, 1890)

Magee, Elizabeth, *Richard Wagner and the Nibelungs* (Oxford, 1990)

Map, Walter, trans. Tupper, Frederick & Ogle, Marbury Bladen, *De Nugis Curialium (Courtiers' Trifles)*, (London, 1924)

Mellinkoff, Ruth, *Averting Demons*, 2 vols (Los Angeles, 2004)

Mermaids, exhibition catalogue (Københavns Bymuseum, 1973)

Miller, William S., *The Mythology of Milton's* Comus (New York, 1988)

Milton, John, ed. Prince, F.T., *Comus*, in *Comus and other Poems* (Oxford, 1968) 35–82

—, *Paradise Lost*, in *The Poetical Works of John Milton* (London, 1877) 43–279

Montgomerie, N. and W., *The Well at the World's End* (1956)

Morgan, Elaine, *The Descent of Woman* (London, 1989) [1972]

Morgan, Mary, *A Tour to Milford Haven, in the year* 1791 (London, 1795)

Morison, Samuel Eliot, ed. & trans., *Journals and Other Documents on the Life and Voyages of Christopher Columbus* (New York, 1963)

Moule, Thomas, *The Heraldry of Fish: Notices of the Principal Families Bearing Fish in their Arms* (London, 1842)

Newell, Stephanie, 'J.M. Stuart-Young of Onitsha', *Africa*, Vol. 73, No. 4 (London & Edinburgh, 2003) 505–30

Der Nibelungen Noth, ed. Gustav Pfizer, illus. Julius Schnorr von Carolsfeld & Eugen Neureuther (Stuttgart, 1843)

The Nibelungenlied, trans. A.T. Hatto (London, 2004) [1965, revised 1969]

O'Donovan, John (ed.), *Annals of the Kingdom of Ireland*, 7 vols (Dublin, 1851)

Ó hÓgáin, Dáithí, *The Lore of Ireland* (Cork, 2006)

O'Sullivan, Sean, *The Folklore of Ireland* (London, 1974)

Okada, Hiroshige, 'Inverted Exoticism? Monkeys, Parrots, and Mermaids in Andean Colonial Art', in *The Virgin, Saints, and Angels: South American Paintings* 1600–1825 (Stanford, California, 2006) 67–79

Paracelsus [Theophrastus of Hohenheim], trans. Hall, Manly P., 'Book of Nymphs, Sylphs, Pygmies, and Salamanders, and Kindred Beings' in *Paracelsus, His Mystical and Medical Philosophy* (Los Angeles, 1964) 67–78

Petrarch, *The Sonnets of Petrarch*, ed. Bergin, Thomas G., (Verona, 1965)

Philpotts, Beatrice, *Mermaids* (Leicester, 1980)

Physiologus, trans. Carlill, James, in *The Epic of the Beast*, ed. William Rose (London & New York, 1924) 153–250

Plato, trans. Llewelyn Davies, John & Vaughan, David James, *The Republic* (Cambridge, 1852)

Pliny, *Natural History*, trans. Rackham, H., 6 vols (London, 2012)

Pontoppidan, Erich, trans. Andreas Berthelson, *The Natural History of Norway* (London, 1755) [1751 in Danish]

Pope, Alexander, *Pope's Odyssey of Homer* (London etc, 1907) [1726]

Powell, James, *Manatees and Dugongs* (Grantown-on-Spey, 2002)

Pushkin, Alexander, trans. Falen, James E., 'Rusalka' in *Alexander Godunov and other Dramatic Works*, (Oxford, 2007) 177–201

Rachewiltz, Siegfried de, *De Sirenibus: An Inquiry into Sirens from Homer to Shakespeare* (New York & London, 1987)

Renard, Louis, *Poissons, écrevisses et crabes . . . que l'on trouve autour des Isles Moluques* (Amsterdam, 1754) [1717] (unnumbered pages)

Rhys, John, *Celtic Folklore: Welsh and Manx*, 2 vols (London, 1980) [1901]

Rodway, Simon, 'Mermaids, Leprechauns, and Fomorians: A Middle Irish Account of the Descendants of Cain', *Cambrian Medieval Celtic Studies*, No. 59 (Aberystwyth, 2010) 1–17

The Romaunt of the Rose (London, 1911)

Roud, Steve, & Bishop, Julia, eds, *The New Penguin Book of English Folk Songs* (London, 2012)

Scoresby, Captain, *The Arctic Regions: Their Situation, Appearances, Climate, and Zoology* (London, 1849?) [1820]

Sidney, Philip, ed. Katherine Duncan-Jones, 'The Defence of Poesy' in *The Major Works* (Oxford, 2002) [1989] 212–50

Silver, Carole G., *Strange and Secret Peoples: Fairies and Victorian Consciousness* (Oxford, 1999)

Stewart, W. Grant, *The Popular Superstitions and Festive Amusements of the Highlanders of Scotland* (Edinburgh, 1823)

[Swan, John], *Speculum Mundi, or, A Glasse Representing the Face of the World*, 3rd edn (London, 1665)

Sylvester, Joshua, 'Of Lovers', in Allott, Robert, *Englands Parnassus* (Menston, 1970) [1600]

Thackeray, William, *Vanity Fair* (London, 1985) [1848]

de Thaun, Philippe, *The Bestiary of Philippe de Thaun*, in *Popular Treatises on Science written during the Middle Ages*, ed. Wright, Thomas (London, 1841) 74–131

Thomson, David, *The People of the Sea* (Edinburgh, 2001) [1954]

Thorpe, Benjamin, *Northern Mythology*, 3 vols (London, 1852)

Turville-Petre, G., *Origins of Icelandic Literature* (Oxford, 1953)

Udovitch, Mim, 'Mariah's World: Inside the nonstop life of a jet-set diva', *Rolling Stone Magazine* 834 (17.2.2000) 42–8

Vermeule, Emily, *Aspects of Death in Early Greek Art and Poetry* (Berkeley, 1979)

Vickers, Lu, & Dionne, Sara, *Weeki Wachee, City of Mermaids* (Gainesville, 2007)

Vinycomb, John, *Fictitious and Symbolic Creatures in Art* (London, 1906)

Virgil, *The Aeneid*, trans. Mackail, J.W. (London, 2004)

Wagner, Richard, trans. Jameson, Frederick, *The Rhinegold* (Mainz, 1900?)

Waugh, Arthur, 'The Folklore of the Merfolk', *Folklore* Vol. 71, June 1960 (London, 1960) 73–84

Weiss, Kenneth, & Buchanan, Anne, *The Mermaid's Tale: Four Billion Years of Cooperation in the Making of Living Things* (Cambridge, Mass, 2009)

Wells, H.G., *The Sea Lady* (Thirsk, 2002) [1902]

Westwood, Jennifer, & Simpson, Jacqueline, *The Lore of the Land* (London, 2005)

Whitbourne, Richard, *A Discourse and Discovery of New-found-land* (London, 1622)

Wilde, Oscar, 'The Fisherman and His Soul', in *A House of Pomegranates* (London, 1891) 63–128

Woodhouse, A.S.P, & Bush, Douglas, *The Minor English Poems*, Vol. 2 of *A Variorum Commentary on the Poems of John Milton*, 6 vols (London, 1972)

Ystad, Vigdis, 'Ibsen, Drachmann and The Lady from the Sea', *Scandinavica: An International Journal of Scandinavian Studies*, Vol. 37, No.2 (Norwich, 1998) 185–96

Index

Acknowledgements

I have had essential help and encouragement from many friends and colleagues, including Katie Fischel, Oscar Fuenzalida, Suzi Hopkins, Pradeep Jey, Iain Lynton, Małgorzata Miśniakiewicz, Caroline Oates, Karina Pereira, Davide Rapacciale, Kristina Rapacki, Graeme Rosie, Ann Shearer, Simona Šiaulytytė, Jacqueline Simpson, Craig Stevenson, Cottia Thorowgood, Hatty Thorowgood, Lourdes Vega-Arregui, and Judy Westacott.

Special thanks to Alan Griffiths, for advice on classical Sirens; Terry Gunnell, for translating from Old Icelandic; Joy Hallam, for showing me her superb collection of mermaids; Jeremy Harte, for invaluable comments on an early draft; and Brynhild Weihe at the Tourist Board of the Faroe Islands, for kindly helping to track down selkie stamps. I am most grateful to Gracie Burnett, Adrian Cooper, Ruth Reisenberger and Graham Shackleton at Little Toller for all their hard work on this book, to Howard Wix, Richard Harms and Will Smith for being the first Little Toller subscribers, and to my agent David Marshall for support throughout.

As for printed sources, this is by no means the first book on the mermaid's history. Gwen Benwell & Arthur Waugh's *Sea Enchantress* (1961) is indispensable, particularly supplemented by Waugh's 1960 article in *Folklore*. For the visual record, there is superb material in Beatrice Philpotts' *Mermaids* (1980) and the catalogue of the 1973 *Mermaids* exhibition in Copenhagen. I have consulted all these on many topics, and have not cited them in the specific references below, but full details are in the bibliography.

Little Toller **Monographs**

Our monograph series is dedicated to new writing attuned to the natural world and which celebrates the rich variety of the places we live in. We have asked a wide range of the very best writers and artists to choose a particular building, plant, animal, myth, person or landscape, and through this object of their fascination tell us wider stories about the British Isles.

The titles

HERBACEOUS *Paul Evans*
ON SILBURY HILL *Adam Thorpe*
THE ASH TREE *Oliver Rackham*
MERMAIDS *Sophia Kingshill*
FELL WALL *Richard Skelton*
BLACK APPLES OF GOWER *Iain Sinclair*

In preparation

LANDFILL *Tim Dee*
RAIN *Melissa Harrison*
MILITARY MOUNTAIN *Horatio Clare*
PEBBLES *Christopher Stocks & Angie Lewin*

A postcard sent to Little Toller will ensure you are put on our mailing list and amongst the first to discover each new book as it appears in the series. You can also follow our latest news at littletoller.co.uk or visit our online magazine theclearingonline.org for new essays, short films and poetry.

LITTLE TOLLER BOOKS
Lower Dairy, Toller Fratrum, Dorset DT2 0EL